MORE
slow
cooker
RECIPES

MORE
slow
cooker
RECIPES

OVER **120** DELICIOUS AND EASY DISHES

Katie Bishop

Collins

Collins
An Imprint of HarperCollins*Publishers*
77–85 Fulham Palace Road,
Hammersmith, London W6 8JB

www.harpercollins.co.uk

Collins is a registered trademark of
HarperCollins*Publishers* Ltd

First published by Collins in 2009

10 9 8 7 6 5 4 3 2 1

A catalogue record of this book is available from the British Library.

ISBN 978-0-00-732559-7

Printed and bound in Great Britain by Martins the Printers,
Berwick-upon-Tweed

Contents

Introduction

'Surely there's a limit to the number of ways you can slow cook something,' said the doubters when I took on this second book of over 100 recipes. Little did they know! Such is the versatility of the slow cooker I had loads of ideas up my sleeve for book two! I hope you enjoy this collection of 130 new recipes, just as lovingly written, tested and devoured as those in book one.

This book is designed to be really simple to use. If you fancy a curry or something spicy then look in the curries section, or maybe rich braises and stews are the reason for your slow cooker's presence in your kitchen, so take a look at that chapter. In my kitchen my slow cookers (cookers are plural because at the last count I had eight!) are a godsend for midweek meals, but particularly when entertaining. I love to have large gatherings and parties, and it is at these times I could not live without a slow cooker. This New Year's Eve we had a house full of guests, so we filled a slow cooker with mulled wine and left it ticking over on the warming function, ready to take the chill off when the guests arrived. There was also a buffet table with two slow cookers – one containing Beef with whole spices and the other with Fruity Moroccan spiced shanks (see pages 72 and 82). They had been thrown together 8 hours before and then left to their own devices while I relaxed and did my nails (!). Both dishes were smart enough to be left *in situ* ready for guests to serve themselves. Entertaining for a large number has never been easier, so if that's your thing, you'll also find a chapter for feasts and celebrations.

One of the areas that I was most excited about experimenting with in this book was 'super slow' cooking. All the top chefs seem to be doing it at the moment with laudable results, so why shouldn't we at home? Well, often we can't, as the temperature on most domestic ovens makes it impossible – many don't go low enough. I guess there's also an element of concern for food safety and waste when 'experimenting' like this at home. With your best interests at heart (and admittedly many of my own) I went about creating a 'super slow' chapter where I would do the experimenting for you – what would happen to the ingredients, would they still taste good and more intense in flavour or would the flavour begin to diminish? Would super slow cooking really, honestly, make a better dish out of an ingredient than if I had just thrown it all in a conventional oven for 2 hours? The unbelievably tasty, gorgeous and sumptuous dishes within this chapter will, I hope, convince you that over a long period of time some ingredients evolve into something even more spectacular than would be achieved with conventional cooking, often with significantly less time-consuming attention and hassle.

There are also yummy chapters on roasts, light and easy dishes, chillies and pasta sauces as well as puddings and cakes. So, whatever your penchant and requirements, whether after-work suppers, make-ahead meals or those days when you just don't want to spend too much time in the kitchen, there should be a chapter for you!

A note on slow cooker sizes

All the recipes in this book have been cooked and tested in a 5.7 litre (10 pint) slow cooker. If your slow cooker is a different size then you will need to adjust the ingredients and cooking times accordingly. If you find that recipes requiring tins or dishes to be placed inside the slow cooker are difficult to follow (because of the size of your slow cooker), then try using individual ramekins or ovenproof dishes instead, and adjust the cooking times accordingly. Please remember that every brand of slow cooker is different, so it's critical to follow the individual manufacturer's instructions.

My guide to slow cooking

If you haven't used a slow cooker before then this section is definitely worth reading. Indeed, if you've been using a slow cooker for a while and are starting to feel a bit bored with the results, then some of these guidelines may just remind you of the many possibilities of your slow cooker and help you expand your repertoire.

What to buy?

There are so many slow cookers on the market it can be difficult to know where to start when buying one. Either way, they are basically made up of a heated, electric element, which surrounds an inner dish with a lid. The cooker is plugged into the mains and controlled simply to high or low.

You will also find options for timers, beepers, lights, digital screens... the list goes on, but for me there are two main factors when choosing a machine: what size is it? And does it have a removable, ovenproof inner dish?

Most major brands will come in a choice of sizes these days. The capacity of your model will depend on the number of people you wish to cook for, and the type of food you want to cook. As a benchmark, a 5–6 litre (9–10½ pint) cooker should easily cater for six people. If you like to cook large batches of food for freezing, or entertaining, then a 6 litre (10½ pint) capacity model or more would be perfect for you. If you would like to cook joints of meat or larger cuts, then try an oval-shaped cooker. Round models tend to be better suited to soups, stews and puddings.

A removable, ovenproof inner dish is a must for me, as the cooker immediately becomes much more versatile; it's also easier to clean and store. An ovenproof inner means that you can use the dish in the oven, if you wish, and makes it more attractive for taking directly to the table. I also find that I have more control when cooking, as I can remove the dish from the heat source immediately if I want to, and I can also grill the top of dishes, if required. Some slow cookers now have inner dishes that are flameproof too, and can be used on the hob, making them even more adaptable.

The important thing to remember is that every machine will be different. They will reach different top temperatures and be suited to different lengths of cooking and techniques. It is essential that you check the manufacturer's instructions for your machine before embarking on any of these recipes or any of your own creations.

It's also worth acknowledging that a slow cooker is completely different from a pressure cooker and will have very different results – they are not comparable, although there seems to be a popular belief that they are one and the same thing.

One of the questions I am asked most about slow cooking is, **'Is it safe?'** Concerns can range from food safety to worries about fire and energy consumption.

The United States Food Safety and Inspection Service states that when slow cooking, 'The direct heat from the pot, lengthy cooking and steam created within the tightly covered container combine to destroy bacteria and make the slow cooker a safe process for cooking foods.'

A slow cooker will operate at about 77–97°C (171–207°F), depending on its selected temperature setting and manufacturer's variations. In England a temperature of 75°C (167°F) is deemed adequate to destroy any harmful bacteria. Once food has reached this temperature, it can be kept at a lower temperature for up to 2 hours and still be consumed safely. So, a slow cooker that has been given time to warm up and reach its optimum temperature at the designated setting will safely destroy the risk of food poisoning. If you are in any doubt, I suggest you stick to cooking pieces of meat, as opposed to whole birds or joints and/or invest in a simple cooking thermometer for inserting into ingredients to test their core temperature.

If I still have to convince you of the safety of your machine, then you can also turn the slow cooker onto high for the first hour of cooking to bring the temperature to above 75°C (167°F). However, I rarely do this, and remain alive to tell the tale! My view is that if you begin with fresh ingredients, use clean utensils and a clean thermometer, there is no reason why you should have any concerns at all about food safety with your slow cooker.

While talking about **safety** it's also important to point out that a slow cooker can be left on for many hours, unattended, but make sure you always follow the manufacturer's instructions for exact environmental safety precautions.

With basic care, using a slow cooker couldn't be simpler. In essence, all you need do is to fill the dish up with ingredients, put the lid on and set it to low or high to begin cooking. That said, there are a few basic principles that I stick to in order to create the best possible recipes.

It's easy to get carried away and **overfill** your slow cooker – aim to fill the inner dish about half full, or ideally no more than two-thirds full, and certainly no more than 4cm (1½in) from the top. Place the ingredients that take the longest time to cook, such as root vegetables and large cuts of meat, on the bottom of the slow cooker dish so they have maximum heat exposure. Less hardy ingredients, such as rice, pasta, dairy products and certain more delicate vegetables, should be added at the end of cooking, usually during the last hour or so.

Resist the temptation to lift the lid of the slow cooker or stir the contents, as doing so will affect the temperature in the cooker and allow all-important moisture to escape during cooking. However, if you find that your slow cooker has 'hot spots', then you may find occasional stirring helpful to encourage even cooking.

Slow cooking affects the flavour of food in a different way to conventional methods. As a result it is a good idea to **season** your food at the end of cooking, unless otherwise stated in the recipe (a common exception would be when cooking certain vegetables, when seasoning can help to concentrate their flavour). When cooking with brown rice, beans or pulses, I always season at the end of cooking, whether slow or conventional, as the salt can toughen the outer husk, making it chewy and less pleasant to eat. It's also a good idea to add soft herbs, such as parsley, basil and mint, towards the end of cooking to avoid their discoloration and loss of flavour.

The flavour of any stew, curry or casserole is undoubtedly enhanced if it is left to cool, chilled overnight and **reheated** the next day (this also allows you to remove some of the fat that will have solidified on the surface). In addition, these foods also tend to **freeze** brilliantly. If you, like me, are a fan of freezing, then there are a few things to consider. Ideally, transfer any leftovers out of the slow cooker to allow them to cool – this will be preferable to cooling them in the already warm slow cooker, which could encourage the growth of bacteria. Store leftovers in shallow, covered containers and refrigerate or freeze within 2 hours of cooking.

Defrost any frozen foods thoroughly in the fridge before reheating. **Never reheat food in your slow cooker** as it will not reach a safe temperature for long enough. Cooked foods should be reheated on the hob, in a microwave or in a conventional oven until piping hot. The hot food can then be placed in a preheated slow cooker to keep it hot for serving, if you wish.

Never use **frozen ingredients** in your slow cooker. The heat in your slow cooker is likely to be unevenly distributed, which could result in some ingredients not reaching a safe and hygienic temperature. It would also create a lot of excess liquid, which a slow cooker is ill-equipped to get rid of.

The ceramic insert in a slow cooker can crack if exposed to sudden **temperature changes**, so it's a good idea not to put a ceramic slow cooker dish into a preheated base straight from the fridge. Equally avoid putting a hot slow cooker dish directly onto a cold surface, even if that surface is heatproof.

Your slow cooker will cope admirably if you throw some ingredients in and leave it to its own devices. However, when cooking with meat and vegetables, and if you have plenty of time, you might like to **brown** them first. This will give the dish extra colour as well as flavour. In addition, it will render fattier cuts of meat, removing some excess fat, which is healthier for us and can also result in a better dish. In my recipes, however, I am always conscious of saving time, so I only include browning if it makes a significant difference to the finished dish.

For more even cooking, **trim excess fat** from meats, as high-fat foods cook more quickly than other ingredients, such as vegetables. If you're making a recipe with both meat and root vegetables, it is often a good idea to make a bed of vegetables on the bottom of the dish and place the meat on top, so that it cooks evenly. Saying that, foods high in fat aren't necessarily a bad thing for slow cooking. This 'good' fat comes from intramuscular fat running through certain cuts of meat, as opposed to the layer of fat on the surface of meat. For more information see the specific advice on meat on page 15.

Slow cooking does not allow for the evaporation that occurs in other cooking methods, so it is advisable to reduce the amount of **liquid** you would usually use in conventional recipes. You can usually do this by up to 50 per cent, although as a general rule of thumb I use about one-third less liquid than in my conventional recipes. If you want a thicker, less watery sauce try removing the lid and increasing the setting to high to allow for some of the excess to evaporate. Alternatively, transfer the sauce to a saucepan and boil over a high heat for a much faster reduction method. You could also sprinkle a little plain flour over the ingredients in the slow cooker dish before cooking to achieve a thicker sauce.

Baking in a slow cooker defies many regular rules, but it is possible. I either grease and line the slow cooker dish thoroughly with butter and baking parchment or use an ovenproof dish or dishes and use the slow cooker as a water bath (also called a *bain marie*). Both methods work well and are suited to light cakes and sponges, and especially custards and similar dishes. Please see page 16 for more guidance on cooking with dairy products. Your manufacturer's instructions will also give you a further indication of your machine's suitability for baking. In most cases you will need to preheat the slow cooker and may need to cook on high if you are using raising agents. Check individual recipes for specific guidelines.

Personal preference and differences in slow cooker models will always create variations in cooking times and temperatures. However, most recipes can be **adapted** for slow cooking. Simply follow the guidelines above and cook until tender. As a basic rule of thumb, a recipe that cooks for 1½–2 hours on the hob will probably take about 4 hours on high in the slow cooker. This would translate to 8 hours on the low setting. I generally prefer cooking on the low setting (unless baking, when I need a higher temperature to make things rise), as I feel the longer time period coaxes out even more flavour from the ingredients. It also ensures more even, thorough cooking.

You can cook almost anything in a slow cooker, but for the best results choose **the right ingredients**. At its most basic, every good stew or casserole includes one or more of the flavour-enhancing ingredients, such as onions, shallots, leeks or celery, and maybe a selection of root vegetables, perhaps floury potatoes, turnips, swedes, parsnips or carrots.

When it comes to **meat**, even the most coarse cuts of meat can be trans-formed into meltingly soft, flavoursome delights! All you need is time and a few additional ingredients and the magic of slow cooking will do the rest.

To get the most from any cut of meat it must be 'fit for purpose' or cooked appropriately. Lean, fine-grained cuts respond well to fast, high-temperature cooking, while tougher cuts with more connective tissue need long, slow cooking to make them tender.

For me, knowing how to use and get the best from a whole carcass is something that every carnivorous cook should know about. You'll get the best, most varied eating experience, but vitally it makes the best economic sense – for cooks, butchers and farmers alike.

Generally the slow cook cuts come from the parts of the animal that have to work the hardest – the forequarter (neck, belly, shoulders) and the legs. These tough, sinewy muscles will taste dreadful if they are not cooked correctly, but so too would the finest fillet of beef. Using a moist method of cooking, or cooking these cuts in some well-seasoned liquid – whether it is stock, wine or even water – will work wonders. The liquid will encourage the muscles to relax their tough structure, and the gelatine that this process produces will, in turn, flavour the liquid to make wonderful gravy. Not only do these cuts present tremendous value for money, but they also taste great. It is also worth considering that cuts labelled 'stewing' will usually take longer to tenderise than those labelled 'braising'.

Dried beans still need to be soaked overnight before slow cooking. Dried red kidney beans must also be boiled for at least 10 minutes and drained before cooking to remove their dangerous toxins. Other pulses – such as lentils and canned beans – can be used directly, but will break up with a very extended period of cooking.

Pasta and rice should be added to moist, saucy recipes in the slow cooker about 30–50 minutes before the end of cooking. Baked pasta and risotto dishes also work very well (see pages 31 and 33 for some great ideas).

Dairy products such as milk, cheese, cream and yoghurt tend to break down in the slow cooker after prolonged cooking (over 6 hours). However, they can be used either for a shorter period of time or stirred in at the end (the last hour) of cooking to finish a dish.

1

Light dishes

Spinach and lentil soup

PREPARATION TIME: 15 MINUTES
COOKING TIME: 3-4 HOURS
SERVES 4

This colourful, hearty soup is packed with flavour. You can use either chicken or vegetarian stock.

75g (3oz) brown or green lentils
Olive oil
1 garlic clove, peeled
1 red onion, peeled and finely diced
1 celery stick, trimmed and finely diced
1 x 400g (14oz) tin chopped tomatoes

2 fresh thyme sprigs
1 bay leaf, broken
2 litres (3½ pints) stock
125g (4½oz) baby spinach leaves
Sea salt and freshly ground black pepper
Extra virgin olive oil or basil oil, for drizzling

Wash the lentils in cold water and drain thoroughly. Pour in 1-2mm (⅟₁₆in) of olive oil to cover the base of the slow cooker dish.

Using your thumb, press the garlic firmly to bruise it, then add it to the dish. Add the lentils and mix to coat in the oil. Add the onion, celery, tomatoes and herbs and mix together. Don't season the soup at this stage, as salt will toughen the lentils. Pour the stock over the lentils. Cover with the lid and cook on high for 3-4 hours or until the lentils are tender.

Using a slotted spoon, remove the garlic and herbs. Mix the spinach into the soup and stir until the leaves are just wilted. Season to taste with salt and pepper.

Ladle the soup into warm bowls and drizzle with a touch of extra virgin olive oil or basil oil before serving with ciabatta.

FAB FOR THE FREEZER
Leave to cool before transferring to freezerproof containers and freezing for up to three months. Defrost thoroughly before reheating gently on the hob (never in the slow cooker).

Spicy celeriac and apple soup

PREPARATION TIME: 10 MINUTES
COOKING TIME: 4 HOURS
SERVES 6   VEGETARIAN

I absolutely love celeriac raw in salads and remoulade, but here it really benefits from long slow cooking, which coaxes out its characteristic nutty flavour. The warming spices of the curry paste and the tart apple also work well to complete this easy soup.

1 large celeriac, about 1.5kg (3lb 5oz), peeled (about 1.3kg/ 2lb 13oz peeled weight) and cut into 3cm (1¼in) chunks
1 large onion, peeled and cut into 3cm (1¼in) chunks
1 cooking apple, peeled, cored and diced
Juice of 1 lemon
2 vegetable stock cubes
1 tbsp medium curry paste
1 litre (1¾ pints) boiling water
Sea salt and freshly ground black pepper

Place the celeriac and onion chunks in the slow cooker dish. Add the diced apple, then pour over the lemon juice and toss together until everything is coated in the juice.

Place the stock cubes and curry paste into a large measuring jug, then pour over the boiling water and stir to dissolve the cubes. Pour this mixture over the celeriac and top up with more boiling water if the vegetables and apple are not covered with liquid (otherwise the apple with turn brown). Cover with the lid and cook on high for 4 hours or until the vegetables are completely tender.

Remove the slow cooker dish from the heated base and place it on a heatproof surface. Blitz the soup with a hand-held blender until completely smooth (or blend in batches in a food processor). Add more hot stock if you like your soup thinner. Season to taste with salt and pepper and serve.

I ALSO LIKE...
making this soup with parsnips instead of celeriac.

Chicken and lemon soup

PREPARATION TIME: 5 MINUTES
COOKING TIME: 6½–8½ HOURS
SERVES 4

Slow cooking the chicken on the bone before adding it to the soup gives it a wonderful flavour.

750g (1lb 10oz) chicken wings
1 celery stick, trimmed and finely
   diced
1 leek, trimmed and finely diced
1 garlic clove, peeled and crushed
1 fresh lemon thyme sprig, plus
   extra to garnish (or use 1
   ordinary thyme sprig)

Finely grated zest and juice of
   1 lemon (preferably unwaxed)
1 large potato, peeled and cut
   into small 1cm (½in) cubes
3 tbsp double cream
Sea salt and freshly ground black
   pepper

Place the chicken wings, celery, leek, garlic, thyme and lemon zest and juice into the slow cooker dish and mix well. Cover with the lid and cook on high for 2 hours, stirring halfway through cooking.

After 2 hours, carefully pour enough boiling water into the slow cooker dish to cover the chicken and stir to combine. Cover with the lid again and cook on low for a further 4–6 hours (the longer the better).

Strain the chicken and vegetables through a sieve into a large saucepan. Pick over the chicken, discarding any skin or bone but saving the meat, and add the meat to the pan. Bring to the boil over a high heat, skimming with a slotted spoon to remove any remaining skin, sinew or bits of vegetable that have escaped the straining process.

Add the potato to the soup and simmer for 10 minutes or until the potato is tender. Remove the pan from the heat and stir in the cream. Season to taste with salt and pepper and serve immediately sprinkled with a few lemon thyme leaves.

I ALSO LIKE...
to use baby pasta or risoni (a type of pasta that looks like large grains of rice, used in soups, salads, stews, stuffings, etc.) instead of potato in this soup.

Thai pumpkin soup

PREPARATION TIME: 10 MINUTES

COOKING TIME: 3 HOURS

SERVES 4-6

Butternut squash or pumpkin tastes great in Thai recipes. Here it makes a comforting, smooth soup, which is great for everyday food or as a starter when entertaining.

1.5kg (3lb 5oz) butternut squash or pumpkin, peeled, deseeded and cut into chunks

1 red onion, peeled and diced

2.5cm (1in) piece fresh root ginger, peeled and grated

1-2 tsp red Thai curry paste, or to taste

1 litre (1¾ pints) hot vegetable stock

150ml (5fl oz) coconut milk

1 tbsp lime juice

1 tbsp fish sauce, or to taste

1 tbsp demerara sugar

Fresh coriander leaves, to garnish

Place the butternut squash or pumpkin in the slow cooker dish together with the onion, ginger and curry paste and mix well until the pumpkin is coated. Cover with the lid and cook on high for 2 hours or until the squash is really tender. Remove the slow cooker dish from the base, but leave the slow cooker switched on.

Place the squash or pumpkin and any cooking juices into a food processor and blitz, adding a little of the hot stock to loosen the mixture, until smooth. Gradually add the remaining stock.

Return the mixture to the slow cooker dish and add the coconut milk, lime juice and fish sauce. Place the dish back onto the heated base and replace the lid. Cook for 1 hour or until hot.

Season the soup with more fish sauce and the sugar to taste. Ladle into warm bowls and sprinkle with coriander leaves before serving.

I ALSO LIKE...
cooking this recipe to the end of paragraph 1 and then mixing the squash or pumpkin cubes with all the other ingredients except the stock. It's great heated through and served with rice noodles.

Split pea and ham soup

PREPARATION TIME: 5 MINUTES, PLUS OVERNIGHT SOAKING
COOKING TIME: 2-3 HOURS
SERVES 4

This easy soup is very warming and tasty – perfect for a cold day or if you're in need of some real comfort food.

2 tbsp olive oil
2 leeks, white part only, diced
2 garlic cloves, peeled and finely chopped
500g (1lb 2oz) green split peas, soaked overnight and drained
2 litres (3½ pints) chicken or vegetable stock
2 tbsp roughly chopped fresh flat-leaf parsley
50g (2oz) ham, finely shredded

Pour the olive oil into the slow cooker dish, then mix in the leeks, garlic, drained split peas and stock.

Cover with the lid and cook on high for 1 hour. Remove the lid and skim off and discard any froth from the surface with a slotted spoon. Mix the soup well, then cover again and cook for a further 1–2 hours or until the peas are tender.

Ladle the soup into serving bowls and top with the parsley and shredded ham. Serve with hot buttered toast.

I ALSO LIKE...
replacing the ham with hot, crispy bacon pieces.

Mixed mushroom and herb bruschetta

PREPARATION TIME: 5 MINUTES
COOKING TIME: 4 HOURS
SERVES 4   VEGETARIAN

Mushrooms love being slow cooked! The gentle process seems to maximise of their flavour. Use really fresh mushrooms to make the most of their texture and to prevent the mixture from becoming too brown.

500g (1lb 2oz) mixed mushrooms, such as button, cup, Portabella or whatever is in season, wiped clean and cut into large wedges or thick slices

50g (2oz) chilled butter, cut into cubes

2 tbsp olive oil

Sea salt and freshly ground black pepper

Finely grated zest and juice of 1 lemon (preferably unwaxed)

1 garlic clove, peeled

4 tbsp finely chopped fresh herbs, such as parsley, basil, mint and chives, plus extra to garnish

50g (2oz) creamy Italian cheese, such as Taleggio or Dolcelatte, crumbled

8 bruschetta slices or slices of ciabatta

Place the mushrooms in the slow cooker dish (you need to have enough to cover the base of the dish thickly). Add the butter, olive oil, 1 teaspoon of salt, lemon zest and juice.

Cut the garlic clove in half lengthways and finely chop one of the pieces. Add this to the mushrooms and mix everything together well. Cover with the lid and cook on low for about 4 hours or until the mushrooms are tender and much of the liquid has evaporated. Stir in the herbs and cheese, then season to taste with salt and pepper.

About 5–10 minutes before the end of cooking, toast the bread until golden, then rub the cut side of the reserved garlic over the toast. Spoon the hot mushroom mixture over the toast and sprinkle with more herbs to garnish.

I ALSO LIKE...
to toss these creamy mushrooms through hot pasta.

Easy chicken liver pâté

PREPARATION TIME: 10 MINUTES
COOKING TIME: 2¼ HOURS
MAKES 500G (1LB 2OZ) PÂTÉ

I'm a real fan of chicken liver pâté, and it's so economical to make! I like a smooth pâté, but if you prefer, simply process for less time to make a coarse version. This pâté will keep in the fridge for about a week and also freezes really well for a month.

400g (14oz) fresh chicken livers,
  rinsed and drained
1 tbsp butter, plus extra for
  greasing
1 small onion, peeled and finely
  diced
50g (2oz) dried natural
  breadcrumbs

2 tbsp double cream
2 tbsp Marsala or brandy
  (optional)
125g (4½oz) pork mince
2 fresh sage leaves
1 fresh thyme sprig, leaves only
A small pinch of mace

Pick over the livers, trimming any membranes away. Butter a small loaf tin or ovenproof dish that will fit into your slow cooker dish.

Melt the remaining butter in a frying pan over a medium heat. Add the onion and sweat for about 5 minutes or until soft. Remove from the heat and add the breadcrumbs, cream and Marsala or brandy. Set aside for about 5 minutes.

Place the onion, soaked breadcrumbs and all the other ingredients except for one of the sage leaves in a food processor and blitz until it reaches your preferred consistency. Place one of the sage leaves, attractive side down, into the bottom of the prepared tin or dish, then spoon the pâté mixture over the top and level the surface. Cover with a double layer of buttered foil.

Place the tin or dish in the slow cooker dish and carefully pour enough boiling water around the outside to come about one-third of the way up the sides of the tin or dish. Cover with the lid and cook on high for about 2 hours or until firm to the touch. Remove the tin or dish from the slow cooker and leave to cool completely before unwrapping and turning out. Cut into slices and serve with hot toast.

Balsamic beetroot and orange salad

PREPARATION TIME: 10 MINUTES
COOKING TIME: 4–5 HOURS
SERVES 4   VEGETARIAN

This classic combination of flavours is always a winner in our house.

4 raw beetroots, scrubbed

1 garlic clove, peeled and crushed

3 oranges

50ml (1³/₄fl oz) balsamic vinegar

50ml (1³/₄fl oz) extra virgin olive
  oil

A small handful of fresh mint
  leaves

1 tbsp finely diced shallot

150g (5oz) mixed salad leaves,
  such as lamb's lettuce or baby
  leaves

200g (7oz) soft goat's cheese,
  crumbled

50g (2oz) walnut pieces

Trim the roots and green leafy tops from the beetroot, cut them into chunky wedges and place into the slow cooker dish together with the garlic, finely grated zest and juice from one of the oranges, the vinegar and half the olive oil. Cover with the lid and cook on low for 4–5 hours or until tender. Leave to cool completely in the slow cooker.

Using a serrated knife, cut the top and bottom from the remaining oranges. Place them on a board and slice off the peel in downward strips, being careful to remove the pith as well. Then hold one orange in your hand over a small bowl and cut each segment of orange away by cutting between the membranes. Allow the segments and any juice to collect in the bowl.

Finely shred half of the mint leaves. Add the remaining olive oil, chopped mint, shallot and salt and pepper to the orange segments and set aside.

Place the salad leaves on a large platter. Using a slotted spoon, remove the beetroot from its cooking liquid and scatter over the salad. Drizzle over the orange segments and dressing, then scatter with the remaining mint, the goat's cheese and walnuts to serve.

COOKING CONVENTIONALLY?
Wrap the prepared beetroot in foil and cook in an oven preheated to 180°C (350°F), Gas mark 4, for 2–3 hours or until tender.

Braised lentil salad

PREPARATION TIME: 5 MINUTES
COOKING TIME: 3 HOURS
SERVES 4 AS A MAIN SALAD   VEGETARIAN

This simple, rustic salad is packed with flavour and is utterly more-ish. It's great on its own with crusty bread or equally at home as an accompaniment to meat, especially lamb.

4-6 tbsp olive oil
1 garlic clove, peeled
250g (9oz) Umbrian or brown lentils, rinsed and drained
1 celery stick, trimmed and finely diced
2 fresh thyme sprigs, leaves only
1 bay leaf, broken

A large pinch of dried basil
1 litre (1¾ pints) vegetable stock
Extra virgin olive oil, to taste
Sea salt and freshly ground black pepper
15g (½oz) fresh flat-leaf parsley, roughly chopped
Lemon wedges, to serve

Cover the base of the slow cooker dish with the olive oil. Using your thumb, press the garlic firmly to bruise it and add it to the slow cooker dish. Add the lentils, celery and herbs and mix well to coat in the oil.

Pour the stock over the lentils. Cover with the lid and cook on high for 3 hours or until the lentils are tender.

Remove from the heat and leave to cool completely. The mixture will be quite liquid. Season to taste with extra virgin olive oil and salt and pepper. Mix in the parsley before serving with lemon wedges.

Moroccan filled peppers

PREPARATION TIME: 10 MINUTES
COOKING TIME: 1½–2 HOURS
SERVES 4   VEGETARIAN

Peppers and slow cooking go hand in hand – the long, gentle process brings out the best in the taste of the peppers. This is a great recipe for a mid-week supper or as a starter when entertaining.

4 red peppers
2 garlic cloves, peeled and finely
   sliced
6 tbsp couscous
3 tbsp boiling water
4 tbsp finely chopped fresh
   herbs, such as basil, flat-leaf
   parsley or mint

3 tbsp olive oil, plus extra for
   drizzling
2 tomatoes, diced
1 tsp harissa paste
Sea salt and freshly ground black
   pepper

Using a sharp knife, halve the peppers, attempting to cut along the centre of the stalk so that each half has a piece of stalk attached to it. Carefully remove the seeds, leaving the stalks intact, and arrange the peppers in a single layer in the slow cooker dish (they should fit snugly with few gaps between them). Divide the garlic slices between the peppers.

Place the couscous in a large bowl and add the boiling water. Add the herbs, olive oil, tomatoes and harissa paste, then season with salt and pepper and mix well. Spoon the mixture neatly into the pepper halves and drizzle a little more olive oil over the top. Cover with the lid and cook on high for 1½–2 hours or until the peppers are wonderfully soft but still holding their shape, and the couscous is tender. Serve immediately with some rocket leaves and dollops of Greek yoghurt.

I ALSO LIKE...
to do this with other vegetables, such as halved, hollowed-out courgettes, tomatoes and mini aubergines, using their diced flesh in the couscous stuffing mixture.

Roasted red pepper, tomato and feta salad

PREPARATION TIME: 15 MINUTES

COOKING TIME: 2–3 HOURS

SERVES 4   VEGETARIAN

This salad is packed full of flavour. It is utterly wonderful in the summer, and particularly good for picnics and barbecues, or just as good for brightening up grey days in winter!

4 red peppers
500g (1lb 2oz) baby cherry
   tomatoes
1 garlic clove, peeled and finely
   chopped
Sea salt and freshly ground black
   pepper
4 handfuls of rocket leaves
200g (7oz) feta cheese, cubed
50g (2oz) toasted pine nuts
Extra virgin olive oil, for drizzling

Using a sharp knife, deseed the peppers and cut each one into 6 wedges. Add the peppers, tomatoes and garlic to the slow cooker dish and season generously with salt and pepper. Cover with the lid and cook on high for 2–3 hours or until softened.

Mix the rocket leaves into the pepper mixture and season to taste. Spoon the pepper mixture onto a platter, then scatter over the feta and pine nuts. Drizzle with a little olive oil and serve with warmed pitta bread.

I ALSO LIKE...
to let this mixture go cold before tossing it through cooked and cooled pasta to make a perfect summer pasta salad.

Braised fennel

PREPARATION TIME: 10 MINUTES

COOKING TIME: 2–3 HOURS

SERVES 2 AS A MAIN COURSE OR 4 AS A SIDE DISH   VEGETARIAN

I love fennel, raw and shaved thinly into a salad, or even more so when braised long and slow until meltingly soft. This recipe is fabulous on its own with crusty bread or as an accompaniment to meat or fish.

4 medium fennel bulbs
2 tbsp olive oil
50g (2oz) butter
75ml (2½fl oz) dry white wine
Zest and juice of ½ lemon
2 bay leaves, broken in half
Sea salt and freshly ground black
pepper

Using a sharp knife, remove the stalks and any damaged outer leaves from the fennel and slice the bulbs in half lengthways. Remove any feathery fronds and set aside.

Pour the olive oil into the slow cooker dish, tipping the dish to ensure an even layer of oil over the base, and arrange the fennel, cut side down, in a single layer in the dish. Dot the top of the fennel with butter and add the wine, lemon zest and juice. Tuck the bay leaves in between the bulbs and season with salt and pepper. Cover with the lid and cook on high for 2–3 hours or until the fennel is soft and the juices have reduced.

Remove the bulbs from the heat and leave to rest for 5–10 minutes. Scatter the reserved fronds over the top before serving.

I ALSO LIKE...
topping the raw fennel with a pork shoulder or belly joint then cooking on low for 6–8 hours until there is no more pink meat, for a delicious all-in-one roast.

Aubergine and tomato bake

PREPARATION TIME: 10 MINUTES
COOKING TIME: 3 HOURS 10 MINUTES
SERVES: 6

Aubergines and tomatoes are a fantastic pairing. Here they are used in an easy, layered bake, which benefits from its long slow cooking in terms of flavour and texture.

3 large aubergines
500g (1lb 2oz) jar good-quality tomato pasta sauce
3 tbsp extra virgin olive oil
A large handful of fresh basil leaves, plus extra to serve
Sea salt and freshly ground black pepper

75g (3oz) quartered black olives
100g (3½oz) grated mozzarella cheese
6 tbsp finely grated fresh Parmesan cheese

Using a sharp knife, trim the aubergines and slice them lengthways into thin slices no wider than a pound coin (about 3mm/⅛in).

Spread about 4 heaped tablespoons of pasta sauce over the base of the slow cooker dish, then top with a third of the aubergine slices and drizzle with some of the olive oil, add a layer of basil and season to taste with salt and pepper. Sprinkle over a third of the olives and a third of the cheeses. Repeat this process twice more, but do not add the final layer of cheese. Finish with the remaining pasta sauce, spreading it evenly over the aubergine slices. Cover with the lid and cook on high for 3 hours or on low for 6 hours until the aubergines are meltingly tender.

Uncover and sprinkle with the reserved mozzarella and Parmesan, then replace the lid and cook on high for a further 10 minutes or until melted. Serve with a dressed green salad.

I ALSO LIKE...
to add a couple of layers of lasagne sheets to this recipe to make a more substantial dish. See the lasagne recipe opposite for more guidance on quantities and how to do it.

Easy mushroom and Parma ham lasagne

PREPARATION TIME: 5 MINUTES
COOKING TIME: 4½–6½ HOURS, PLUS PREHEATING
SERVES 6

This recipe is so easy to make and perfect for a family supper or relaxed entertaining.

A large knob of butter

2 tbsp olive oil

500g (1lb 2oz) sliced white mushrooms

Sea salt and freshly ground black pepper

700g (1lb 9oz) jar good-quality tomato pasta sauce

12 very thin slices of prosciutto di Parma (ham), shredded into 1–2cm (½–¾in) pieces

About 9 sheets white 'no need to pre-cook' dried lasagne

150g (5oz) grated mozzarella cheese

25g (1oz) freshly grated Parmesan cheese

Remove the slow cooker dish from the base and rub the butter generously over the inside of the dish. Turn the slow cooker base (without the dish in it) on to high to preheat.

Warm the olive oil in large frying pan over a high heat. When very hot, add the mushrooms and season generously with salt and pepper. Cook for 5 minutes, stirring occasionally, until the mushrooms are golden. Add the pasta sauce to the pan. Fill the jar a third full with cold water and rinse out the contents into the pan. Add the ham and mix well.

Spread about 4 tablespoons of the mushroom sauce over the base of the slow cooker dish. Top with 3 sheets of the lasagne, about a third of the remaining sauce and a third of the cheeses. Repeat this process twice more but do not cover with the final layer of cheese (the top layer should be the mushroom sauce). Insert the dish carefully into the preheated slow cooker base, cover with the lid and cook on low for 4–6 hours or until the pasta is tender when tested with the tip of a knife.

Once cooked, remove the lid and sprinkle over the reserved cheese. Leave uncovered for about 10–15 minutes or until the cheese has melted. Serve with a dressed green salad.

Sweet and sour sticky ribs

PREPARATION TIME: 15 MINUTES
TOTAL TIME: 6¼-8¼ HOURS
SERVES 4

These tasty pork ribs are so easy to make and lip-smackingly tasty!

150g (5oz) tomato ketchup
150g (5oz) soft dark brown sugar
100ml (3½fl oz) cider vinegar
1 heaped tsp English mustard
  powder
½ tsp paprika
Sea salt and freshly ground black
  pepper
1.5kg (3lb 5oz) individual pork
  ribs

Place the ketchup, sugar, vinegar, mustard powder and paprika into the slow cooker dish, season well with salt and pepper and mix until smooth. Add the ribs and toss to coat evenly in the sauce. Cover with the lid and cook on low for 6–8 hours.

Remove the ribs from the slow cooker and cover with a tent of foil to keep warm. Skim off any excess fat from the surface of the sauce with a spoon and discard. Pour the sauce into a saucepan and bring to the boil over a high heat. Boil for 5 minutes or until thickened, then drizzle over the ribs before serving.

COOKING CONVENTIONALLY?
Preheat the oven to 170°C (325°F), Gas mark 3. Place the ribs into a large casserole dish with a tight-fitting lid and add 250ml (9fl oz) cold water to the sauce ingredients. Cover and bake in the oven for 2½–3 hours or until tender.

Tomato and rocket risotto

PREPARATION TIME: 5 MINUTES
COOKING TIME: 2 HOURS 10 MINUTES
SERVES 4

This risotto is SO easy to make – there's no standing over a pot stirring for ages. Instead everything is mixed together and then left to its own devices.

4 tbsp good-quality olive oil
1 onion, peeled and finely diced
1 garlic clove, peeled and crushed
25g (1oz) butter
250g (9oz) risotto rice
750ml (1¼ pints) chicken or
   vegetable stock

1 x 400g (14oz) tin chopped
   tomatoes
25g (1oz) freshly grated Parmesan
   cheese, plus extra to serve
Sea salt and freshly ground black
   pepper
2 handfuls of rocket leaves

Warm a quarter of the olive oil in a frying pan over a medium–low heat. When hot, add the onion and garlic and sweat gently without colouring for about 5 minutes.

Cover the base of the slow cooker dish with the remaining olive oil. Place the cooked onion and garlic into the dish together with the butter, rice, stock and tomatoes and mix well. Cover with the lid and cook on low for 2 hours or until the rice has absorbed the liquid. Don't be tempted to stir or remove the lid.

Stir in the Parmesan and season to taste with salt and pepper. Fold the rocket through the risotto and serve with plenty of Parmesan to sprinkle over.

COOKING CONVENTIONALLY?
Follow the recipe using a large casserole dish with a tight-fitting lid instead of the slow cooker dish. Add 250ml (9fl oz) cold water before cooking in an oven preheated to 180°C (350°F), Gas mark 4, for 1 hour or until tender, then stir in the rocket and Parmesan and serve.

Warm tomato and olive caponata

PREPARATION TIME: 5 MINUTES

COOKING TIME: 4 HOURS

SERVES 6 AS AN ACCOMPANIMENT   VEGETARIAN

The gentle heat in slow cooking encourages all the wonderful flavours and sweetness out of these ingredients. This dish is rather like an Italian ratatouille and is great with fish and meat as an accompaniment, or as a meal in itself with pasta or a baked potato.

2 large aubergines, cut into chunks

3 celery sticks, trimmed and finely diced

1 onion, peeled and finely diced

1 tbsp baby capers in brine, drained

75g (3oz) stoned olives

25g (1oz) caster sugar, plus extra to taste

150g (5oz) concentrated tomato purée

4 tbsp red wine vinegar

Sea salt and freshly ground black pepper

3 tbsp cold water

Add the vegetables to the slow cooker dish with the capers, olives, sugar, tomato purée, vinegar, ¼ teaspoon of salt and the water and mix well. Cover with the lid and cook on high for 4 hours or until softened and tender.

Season to taste with more sugar and salt and pepper before serving.

COOKING CONVENTIONALLY?
Cook in an ovenproof casserole dish with a tight-fitting lid for 1 hour in an oven preheated to 170°C (325°F), Gas mark 3.

2

Chillies and pasta sauces

Quick tomato sauce

PREPARATION TIME: 5 MINUTES
COOKING TIME: 10–15 HOURS
SERVES 6   VEGETARIAN

This sauce might be slow cooked, but in terms of the preparation involved it is most definitely a 'quick' sauce in my book! The slow cooker then does the rest of the work, drawing out all the sweetness in the tomatoes to make a fabulously rich sauce.

2 x 400g (14oz) tins chopped
  tomatoes
1 small onion, peeled and diced
2 garlic cloves, peeled and
  crushed
4 tbsp olive oil, plus extra to taste

A large pinch of dried oregano
A small pinch of dried basil
A pinch of cayenne pepper
½ tsp sea salt
Freshly grated Parmesan cheese,
  to serve

Place the tomatoes, onion, garlic, olive oil, herbs, cayenne pepper and salt into the slow cooker dish. Cover with the lid and cook for 10–15 hours or until thick and rich.

Season to taste with more salt and pepper and olive oil. And that's it! Spoon over hot pasta with plenty of grated Parmesan cheese to serve.

I ALSO LIKE...
to make a big batch of this sauce and freeze in portions for a quick meal, any time.

Creamy roasted garlic and rocket pasta sauce

PREPARATION TIME: 2 MINUTES
COOKING TIME: 2½–3 HOURS, PLUS COOKING THE PASTA
SERVES 4   VEGETARIAN

Slow cooking garlic makes it sweet and flavoursome – perfect in a creamy pasta dish like this.

1 whole head of garlic, unpeeled
100ml (3½fl oz) white wine
8 tbsp double cream
1 egg yolk
Sea salt and freshly ground black
  pepper

400g (14oz) dried pasta, such as
  farfalle or fusilli
50g (2oz) rocket leaves

Place the whole garlic in the slow cooker dish and pour the wine over the top. Cover with the lid and cook on low for 2½–3 hours, adding more wine if it starts to boil dry, until the garlic is soft.

Using a sharp knife, cut the top from the garlic to expose the tips of the cloves. Squeeze out the softened flesh into a bowl and mash with a fork until smooth. Add the cream together with any juices from the slow cooker dish, then beat in the egg yolk. Season to taste with salt and pepper.

Bring a large saucepan of salted water to the boil. Add the pasta and cook according to the packet instructions or until firm to the bite (*al dente*). Drain the pasta, leaving a little of the cooking water (about 2 tablespoons) behind in the pan. Return the drained pasta to the pan and add the garlic sauce and rocket. Fold through quickly (to avoid making scrambled egg!) to combine and season to taste. Serve with a tomato and red onion salad.

COOKING CONVENTIONALLY?
Wrap the garlic in a double layer of foil, drizzling in a little white wine before sealing. Roast in an oven preheated to 170°C (325°F), Gas mark 3, for 2 hours or until tender and soft.

Peperonata (tomato and red pepper sauce)

PREPARATION TIME: 10 MINUTES
COOKING TIME: 8–10 HOURS
SERVES 6   VEGETARIAN

This thick sauce or stew is really easy to make. This recipe uses tinned tomatoes, but if it's summer and you have lots of fresh tomatoes that need eating, simply peel, deseed and chop about ten and use those instead.

8 red peppers, deseeded and cut
  into strips
2 x 400g (14oz) tins chopped
  tomatoes
1 large onion, peeled and diced
1 garlic clove, peeled and crushed

A large pinch of dried basil
4 tbsp olive oil
Sea salt and freshly ground black
  pepper
Caster sugar, to taste

Place the pepper strips in the slow cooker dish together with the tomatoes, onion, garlic, basil and olive oil. Season to taste with salt and pepper. Cover with the lid and cook on low for 8–10 hours or until thick and rich.

Taste and add more seasoning if necessary, and a little sugar. Serve with crusty bread and a dressed green salad, or spoon over hot pasta.

I ALSO LIKE...
to make a large batch and keep the stew in the fridge – it will keep for about a week packed into a jar and sealed with a layer of olive oil.

Italian tomato and aubergine sauce

PREPARATION TIME: 10 MINUTES
COOKING TIME: 6¼–8¼ HOURS
SERVES 4   VEGETARIAN

One of my lasting memories of Sicily was the classic *sugo alla Norma* (tomato and aubergine sauce). This is my version.

- 1 tbsp olive oil, plus extra to serve
- 1 small onion, peeled and chopped
- 1 garlic clove, peeled and crushed
- 1 green pepper, deseeded and cut into 2cm (³⁄₄in) chunks
- 2 large aubergines, about 450g (1lb), trimmed and cut into 2cm (³⁄₄in) chunks
- 1 x 400g (14oz) tin chopped tomatoes

- 1 tbsp baby capers, rinsed and drained
- 100ml (3½fl oz) red wine
- 1 tsp dried oregano
- Sea salt and freshly ground black pepper
- 150-200g (5-7oz) freshly cooked penne pasta
- A large handful of fresh basil leaves
- Ricotta cheese, to serve (optional)

Warm a large frying pan over a high heat. When hot, add the olive oil, onion and garlic and cook for 5 minutes or until softened but not coloured. Transfer to the slow cooker dish.

Stir the pepper and aubergine chunks into the slow cooker dish with the tomatoes, capers, wine, oregano and seasoning to taste. Cover with the lid and cook for 6-8 hours or until rich and thick.

Taste and add more seasoning if necessary, and drizzle with extra olive oil to taste. Add the cooked drained pasta to the slow cooker dish and mix well. Scatter with the basil leaves and serve with plenty of ricotta (if using) and freshly ground black pepper.

I ALSO LIKE...

to make this dish and then spoon it into a baking dish, before topping with lots of ricotta and Parmesan cheese and baking in an oven preheated to 190°C (375°F), Gas mark 5, until golden and crisp.

Pumpkin and Parmesan pasta sauce

PREPARATION TIME: 10 MINUTES
COOKING TIME: 3-4 HOURS, PLUS COOKING THE PASTA
SERVES 4   VEGETARIAN

This creamy pasta sauce is so easy and economical to make. I love it tossed through pasta, but it also works well as a side dish.

- 1 orange-fleshed pumpkin or butternut squash, peeled, deseeded and diced into 2cm (¾in) chunks
- 1 onion, peeled and finely diced
- 1 red chilli, deseeded and finely diced
- 1 garlic clove, peeled and crushed
- 2 tbsp olive oil
- ¼ tsp ground nutmeg, plus extra to taste
- Sea salt and freshly ground black pepper
- 2 tbsp double cream
- 3 tbsp freshly grated Parmesan cheese
- 100ml (3½fl oz) hot vegetable stock
- 350-400g (12-14oz) penne pasta
- 1 tbsp roughly chopped fresh flat-leaf parsley leaves

Place the pumpkin or squash, onion, chilli, garlic and olive oil into the slow cooker dish together with the nutmeg and some salt and white pepper. Cover with the lid and cook on low for 3-4 hours or until softened.

Place the contents of the slow cooker dish into a food processor, add the cream and two-thirds of the Parmesan cheese and blitz until smooth, gradually drizzling in the hot stock as the motor is running. Season to taste and add more nutmeg if required.

Meanwhile, cook and drain the pasta according to the instructions on the packet. Toss the sauce with the hot pasta and sprinkle over the remaining Parmesan cheese and the chopped parsley. Serve with plenty of freshly ground black pepper.

I ALSO LIKE...

to vary this recipe to make a risotto. Cook the pumpkin to the end of paragraph 1, add 350g (12oz) risotto rice and 1.5 litres (2½ pints) vegetable stock, cover and cook on low for 1½-2 hours, without stirring or uncovering, until tender.

Marinara tomato and seafood pasta sauce

PREPARATION TIME: 5 MINUTES
COOKING TIME: 8½–12½ HOURS
SERVES 4

This easy sauce is a great store-cupboard standby in our house as I usually have prawns or mixed seafood in the freezer and always have a cupboard full of the other ingredients. Always defrost the seafood thoroughly before using.

2 x 400g (14oz) tins chopped
  tomatoes
1 small onion, peeled and finely
  diced
2 garlic cloves, peeled and
  crushed
1 tsp sea salt
1 tbsp caster sugar
100ml (3½fl oz) white wine
60ml (2fl oz) extra virgin olive oil
400g (14oz) mixed cooked
  seafood

TO SERVE
Freshly cooked pasta
Fresh basil leaves

Place the tomatoes, onion, garlic, salt, sugar and wine in the slow cooker dish. Drizzle over half of the olive oil and mix well. Cover with the lid and cook on low for 8–12 hours or until rich and thick.

Increase the heat to high, stir in the seafood, cover again and cook for a further 30 minutes or until piping hot.

Taste and add more seasoning if necessary, and mix in the remaining olive oil. Spoon over hot, freshly cooked pasta, such as spaghetti or tagliatelle, then sprinkle over basil leaves to serve.

SOMETHING DIFFERENT?
If you like spicy food, try adding a whole dried chilli to the sauce at the start of cooking.

Chickpea and sweet potato chilli

PREPARATION TIME: 10 MINUTES
COOKING TIME: 4–5 HOURS
SERVES 4   VEGETARIAN

This colourful vegetarian chilli looks and tastes fantastic. If you like your food spicy, leave the chilli seeds in.

Warm the olive oil in a large frying pan over a medium heat. When hot, add the chilli, garlic and ginger and cook for 30 seconds or until softened but not coloured. Add the

2 tbsp olive oil

1 large red chilli, deseeded and finely chopped

1 garlic clove, peeled and finely chopped

2.5cm (1in) piece fresh root ginger, peeled and finely chopped

1 large red onion, peeled and cut into 2cm (³⁄₄in) pieces

2 red peppers, deseeded and cut into 2cm (³⁄₄in) pieces

½ tsp ground cumin

2 sweet potatoes, about 350g (12oz) each, peeled and cut into 2cm (³⁄₄in) pieces

1 x 410g tin chickpeas, rinsed and drained

2 tbsp orange juice

2 tbsp soured cream, plus extra to serve

Sea salt and freshly ground black pepper

4 tbsp chopped fresh coriander

onion, peppers and cumin and cook, stirring frequently, until softened but not coloured. Tip the mixture into the slow cooker dish, add the sweet potatoes, chickpeas and orange juice and stir well. Cover with the lid and cook on low for 4–5 hours or until the potato is tender.

Before serving, gently stir in the soured cream and season to taste with salt and pepper, being careful not to squish the sweet potatoes. Sprinkle over the coriander and serve with extra soured cream and flour tortillas.

COOKING CONVENTIONALLY?

Cook in an ovenproof casserole dish with a tight-fitting lid for 3 hours in an oven preheated to 150°C (300°F), Gas mark 2.

Italian sausage and red wine ragout

PREPARATION TIME: 10 MINUTES
COOKING TIME: 4¼–6¼ HOURS, PLUS COOKING THE PASTA
SERVES 4

This tasty dish is great for a mid-week supper, or served from a large platter when entertaining at home.

400g (14oz) (about 6) fresh Italian sausages (most major supermarkets have an Italian variety in their sausage selection)
2 tbsp olive oil
1 tsp fennel seeds
1 red onion, peeled, halved and finely sliced
2 garlic cloves, peeled and crushed
1 x 400g (14oz) tin chopped tomatoes
2 tbsp concentrated tomato purée
1 bay leaf, broken
A small pinch of dried basil

100ml (3½fl oz) red wine
350g (12oz) dried pasta, such as tagliatelle or spaghetti
2 tbsp chopped fresh flat-leaf parsley
Sea salt and freshly ground black pepper
Parmesan cheese, to serve

Squeeze the sausage meat out of the sausage skins and roll the contents of each one into 6–7 little balls.

Pour half of the olive oil into the slow cooker dish. Warm the remainder in a large frying pan over a high heat, and when hot add the fennel and cook for about 30 seconds or until fragrant. Add the sausage balls to the hot frying pan and cook until browned all over. Using a slotted spoon transfer the sausage balls to the slow cooker dish.

Continued overleaf

Add the onion to the slow cooker dish together with the garlic, tomatoes, tomato purée, bay leaf, basil and wine. Cover with the lid and cook on low for 4–6 hours. Don't be tempted to remove the lid during cooking.

When you are ready to eat, cook the pasta in a large saucepan of boiling, salted water according to the packet instructions or until firm to the bite (*al dente*). Drain the pasta, leaving a little of the cooking water (about 2 tablespoons) behind in the pan. Tip the pasta and reserved water into the sausage sauce and fold through together with the parsley. Season to taste with salt and pepper. Serve with a block of Parmesan cheese to grate over the top.

FAB FOR THE FREEZER
This sauce freezes really well and will keep for up to three months. Make sure you defrost it thoroughly before gently reheating on the hob (never in the slow cooker). Serve with freshly cooked pasta.

Four bean chilli

PREPARATION TIME: 5 MINUTES

COOKING TIME: 6¼ HOURS

SERVES 6–8   VEGETARIAN

This vegetarian chilli uses tinned beans so it is really easy to make. Vary the beans depending on what you prefer, and always have a few tins in the cupboard.

1 x 400g (14oz) tin butter beans

1 x 400g (14oz) tin red kidney beans

1 x 400g (14oz) tin black eye beans

1 x 400g (14oz) tin cannellini beans

25g (1oz) butter

2 tbsp olive oil

1 large onion, peeled and diced

2 garlic cloves, peeled and finely sliced

3 mixed colour peppers, deseeded and diced

1 x 400g (14oz) tin chopped tomatoes

1 tsp chilli powder, or to taste

2 tsp ground cumin

1 tsp ground coriander

1 tsp dried oregano

350ml (12fl oz) vegetable stock (try to use a low salt variety as salt will toughen the skins of the beans)

2 tbsp soured cream, plus extra to serve

Sea salt and freshly ground black pepper

Place all the beans in a large sieve or colander and rinse under cold running water. Drain well.

Warm a large frying pan over a high heat. When hot, add the butter and olive oil. Once the butter has melted, add the onion and cook, stirring continuously, for 5 minutes or until it starts to soften. Add the garlic and peppers and cook for a further 5 minutes, stirring occasionally until they are softened and starting to colour. Reduce the heat if the vegetables are becoming any more than golden.

Add the vegetables to the slow cooker dish with the drained beans, the tomatoes, spices, oregano and stock. Cover with the lid and cook on low for 6 hours or until thickened.

Stir in the soured cream and season to taste with salt and pepper. Serve with freshly cooked rice and a dollop of soured cream.

Salsa rossa

PREPARATION TIME: 10 MINUTES
COOKING TIME: 6¼–8¼ HOURS, PLUS COOLING
SERVES 4–6

This tasty red sauce is very easy to make and has a great flavour. The radicchio gives the sauce a hint of bitterness that works really well with the sweet red peppers and tomatoes.

2 red peppers

4 tbsp olive oil, plus extra to taste

1 garlic clove, peeled and crushed

1 radicchio lettuce, shredded

1 tsp capers

1 small red chilli, deseeded and finely chopped

2 anchovy fillets, drained and roughly chopped

2 tomatoes, deseeded and diced

Juice of 1 lemon

Sea salt and freshly ground black pepper

A large handful of fresh basil leaves, roughly chopped

A large handful of fresh mint leaves, roughly chopped

Preheat the grill to its highest setting. Place the peppers under the grill and cook until blackened all over. Transfer to a large bowl, cover with cling film and leave to stand for 10 minutes or until cool enough to handle. When cool, peel off the skin under cold running water, then remove and discard the seeds, stalk and any white membrane and cut the flesh into strips.

Place the pepper strips in the slow cooker dish together with any juices. Add the olive oil, garlic, radicchio, capers, chilli, anchovies, tomatoes and lemon juice. Season with salt and pepper and mix well. Cover with the lid and cook for 6–8 hours or until thick and rich.

Add the basil and mint to the slow cooker dish and stir well. Season to taste with more salt, pepper and olive oil and serve with freshly cooked pasta or as a sauce with barbecued meats and fish.

I ALSO LIKE...
to roast the peppers to the end of the first paragraph and then mix with all the remaining ingredients and eat them raw, as a salad.

Veal ragout

PREPARATION TIME: 5 MINUTES
COOKING TIME: 6½–8½ HOURS
SERVES 4

This rich, glossy ragout is packed with flavour and is incredibly easy to make. It makes a lighter alternative to beef mince.

2 tbsp olive oil
1 large red onion, peeled and cut
   into 5mm (¼in) dice
2 celery sticks, (choose the
   darkest green stalks for
   flavour), trimmed and cut into
   5mm (¼in) dice
450g (1lb) minced veal
1 tbsp plain flour

150ml (5fl oz) red wine
4 bay leaves, broken
500ml (18fl oz) hot vegetable
   stock
6 tbsp finely chopped fresh
   flat-leaf parsley
Sea salt and freshly ground black
   pepper

Warm half of the olive oil in a large frying or sauté pan over a medium heat. When hot, add the vegetables and sauté gently, stirring occasionally, for 5 minutes or until softened but not coloured. Spoon into the slow cooker dish.

Return the pan to the heat and increase the temperature to high. When hot, add the remaining olive oil and warm through for a moment before adding the veal. Fry for 8–10 minutes, stirring very occasionally, or until the mince is well browned.

Add the mince to the slow cooker dish and stir in the flour. Add the wine, bay leaves and stock, cover with the lid and cook on low for 6–8 hours or until rich and thick.

Mix in the parsley and season to taste with salt and pepper. Spoon over freshly cooked pappardelle pasta to serve. Great with a dressed green salad.

I ALSO LIKE...
cooking a double batch and freezing in portions for those evenings when I don't have the energy or the inclination to cook.

Mexican mole

PREPARATION TIME: 15 MINUTES
COOKING TIME: 6¼–8¼ HOURS
SERVES 6

Turkey mole is a much-loved Mexican feast day dish.

800g (1lb 12oz) turkey mince
1 tbsp olive oil
1 onion, peeled and diced
2 carrots, peeled and diced
2 celery sticks, trimmed and
  diced
2 bay leaves, broken
2 tbsp concentrated tomato purée
2 tbsp red wine vinegar
1 tsp muscovado sugar, plus extra
  to taste
250ml (9fl oz) chicken stock
50g (2oz) good-quality plain dark
  chocolate (at least 70% cocoa
  solids)

FOR THE SPICE PASTE:
3 red chillies, deseeded and
  chopped
75g (3oz) sesame seeds
50g (2oz) whole blanched
  almonds
50g (2oz) natural peanuts
50g (2oz) raisins
1 tsp coriander seeds
¼ tsp ground cinnamon
12 black peppercorns
6 whole cloves
4 garlic cloves, peeled and
  roughly chopped
2 tbsp cold water

Pat the mince dry with kitchen paper. Warm the olive oil in a large frying pan over a high heat. When hot, add the mince and cook for 5–10 minutes, stirring continuously until well browned. Add the mince to the slow cooker dish together with the onion, carrots, celery, bay leaves, tomato purée, vinegar, sugar and stock, and mix well.

Return the pan to the heat to make the paste. When hot, add the chillies, seeds and nuts and cook for 2–3 minutes or until golden but not browned. Add half the raisins, coriander seeds, cinnamon, peppercorns, cloves and garlic and cook for a further minute or until fragrant. Tip the contents of the frying pan into a food processor and blitz with the water to make a thick paste. Alternatively, use a pestle and mortar.

Mix the paste and the remaining whole raisins with the turkey in the slow cooker dish. Cover with the lid and cook for 6–8 hours or until thick.

Grate the chocolate over the mince mixture and leave to melt in. Stir well and season with more sugar, salt and pepper. Serve with soft flour tortillas and soured cream.

Spinach and lentil soup *see page 18*

(above) **Balsamic beetroot and orange salad** *see page 25*

(right) **Italian sausage and red wine ragout** *see page 43*

(above) **Rogan josh lamb shanks in dark almond sauce** *see page 68*

(left) **Chickpea and sweet potato chilli** *see page 42*

(above) **Chilli-chicken tortillas** *see page 59* • (right) **Beef with whole spices** *see page 72*

Rolled lamb with capers and anchovies *see page 101*

Pork and borlotti bean chilli

PREPARATION TIME: 10 MINUTES
COOKING TIME: 6½–8½ HOURS
SERVES 6

This is a great alternative chilli recipe. Chipotle paste (smoked chilli paste) is available at most good supermarkets and delicatessens.

500g (1lb 2oz) pork shoulder or mince

1 large red onion, peeled and cut into 5mm–1cm (¼–½in) cubes

2 red peppers, deseeded and cut into 5mm–1cm (¼–½in) cubes

2 garlic cloves, peeled and crushed

1–2 tsp of chipotle (smoked chilli) paste or 1 large red chilli, deseeded and finely chopped

1½ tsp ground cumin

1 tbsp concentrated tomato purée

Juice of 1 large orange

150ml (5fl oz) hot chicken or pork stock

2 x 400g (14oz) tins borlotti beans, rinsed and drained

4 tbsp finely chopped fresh coriander

Sea salt and freshly ground black pepper

If you're using pork shoulder cut the meat into small pieces about 5mm–1cm (¼–½in) in size. Place the shoulder or mince into the slow cooker dish together with the onion and peppers. Add the garlic, chipotle paste or chilli, cumin, tomato purée, orange juice and stock and mix well. Cover with the lid and cook on low for 6–8 hours.

Stir in the borlotti beans, cover again and cook on high for a further 30 minutes or until piping hot.

Stir in the coriander and season to taste with salt and pepper. Serve immediately with freshly cooked rice or flour tortillas and soured cream.

COOKING CONVENTIONALLY?

Preheat the oven to 150°C (300°F), Gas mark 2, and cook in an ovenproof casserole dish with a tight-fitting lid with an extra 200ml (7fl oz) cold water for 3 hours or until tender.

Chocolate chilli con carne

PREPARATION TIME: 15 MINUTES
COOKING TIME: 6¾ HOURS
SERVES 4

I love this recipe! The chocolate adds a richness and roundness of flavour to the finished dish.

500g (1lb 2oz) lean beef mince
1 tbsp olive oil
1 large red onion, peeled and diced
1 red pepper, deseeded and diced
2 garlic cloves, peeled and crushed
1 heaped tsp hot chilli powder (or less for a milder chilli)
1 tsp paprika
1 tsp ground cumin
1 beef stock cube

1 x 400g (14oz) tin chopped tomatoes
2 tbsp tomato purée
A pinch of dried thyme
1 x 410g tin red kidney beans, drained and rinsed
1 square of good-quality plain dark chocolate (at least 70% cocoa solids)
Sea salt and freshly ground black pepper

Pat the mince dry with kitchen paper. Warm the olive oil in a large frying pan over a high heat. When hot, add the onion and pepper and cook for 5 minutes or until softened and golden. Add the garlic, chilli, paprika and cumin, stir well and cook, stirring occasionally, for a further 5 minutes. Reduce the heat if anything threatens to burn.

Spoon the vegetables into the slow cooker dish. Return the frying pan to the high heat and, when very hot, add the mince and cook for about 5–10 minutes, stirring well until the mince has broken up and has browned. Spoon the mince into the slow cooker dish.

Crumble the stock cube over the mince and vegetables and mix together with the tomatoes, tomato purée and thyme. Cover with the lid and cook on low for 6 hours or until tender.

Stir in the beans, cover again and cook for a further 30 minutes or until piping hot.

Add the chocolate and season to taste with salt and pepper. Serve with soured cream and plenty of freshly cooked rice.

Picadillo

PREPARATION TIME: 15 MINUTES, PLUS MARINATING (OPTIONAL)
COOKING TIME: 6¼-8¼ HOURS
SERVES 4-6

Picadillo is the original, authentic Mexican sauce; chilli con carne, as much as I love it, is really a Tex-Mex version of it.

250g (9oz) beef mince
250g (9oz) pork mince
1 tbsp red wine vinegar
½ tsp muscovado sugar
Sea salt and freshly ground black pepper
1 tbsp olive oil
1 onion, peeled and finely chopped
2 garlic cloves, peeled and chopped
1 red pepper, deseeded and chopped

2 red chillies, deseeded and chopped
50g (2oz) flaked almonds
50g (2oz) raisins
50g (2oz) stoned green olives, roughly chopped
1 beef or pork stock cube, crumbled
4 tbsp concentrated tomato purée
2 tbsp cold water

Place the mince in a large bowl together with the vinegar, sugar and a generous amount of salt and pepper and mix well. If you have time, leave to marinate in the fridge for an hour.

Warm the olive oil in a large frying pan. When hot, add the onion, garlic, red pepper and chillies and cook for about 5 minutes or until softened and golden. Spoon the vegetables into the slow cooker dish.

Return the frying pan to the heat and add the meat and cook, stirring continuously until well browned. Spoon into the slow cooker dish, add the remaining ingredients and mix well. Cover with the lid and cook on low for 6–8 hours or until thick and rich.

Season to taste with salt and pepper and serve with freshly cooked rice or flour tortillas and plenty of guacamole, soured cream, grated Cheddar cheese and shredded iceberg lettuce.

Proper bolognese

PREPARATION TIME: 10 MINUTES
COOKING TIME: 8¼–10¼ HOURS
SERVES 6

Our friend Neil lived and worked in Italy for a while, and as a result makes the best bolognese ever! Here's my version, using some of his top tips, and a few of my own ideas, to make a slow cooker 'spag bol' that I hope he will love.

2 tbsp olive oil
250g (9oz) pancetta or streaky
  bacon, cut into cubes
1kg (2lb 4oz) coarse ground beef
  mince
250ml (9fl oz) red wine
2 garlic cloves, peeled and
  roughly chopped
500g (1lb 2oz) onions, peeled and
  finely chopped

2 celery sticks, trimmed and
  diced
1 large carrot, peeled and diced
1 x 400g (14oz) tin chopped
  tomatoes
250ml (9fl oz) tomato passata
1 beef stock cube, crumbled
2 bay leaves, broken
Sea salt and freshly ground black
  pepper

Warm the olive oil in a large frying pan over a high heat. When hot, add the pancetta or bacon and cook for 2–3 minutes or until it becomes opaque. Add the mince in batches and cook for 5–10 minutes or until browned, spooning the cooked batches into the slow cooker dish with a slotted spoon as it cooks.

Return the pan to the heat and add the wine. Cook for 1 minute, stirring constantly to scrape any tasty bits from the bottom of the pan. Pour into the slow cooker. Add the garlic, onions, celery, carrot, tomatoes, passata, stock cube and bay leaves to the mince and mix well. Cover with the lid and cook on low for 8–10 hours or until thick and rich.

Season with plenty of salt and pepper and serve with freshly cooked spaghetti. For me, a dressed green salad with plenty of cucumber is essential to go alongside, as well as lots of freshly grated Parmesan cheese and freshly ground black pepper.

I ALSO LIKE...
to make a double batch and freeze in portions. This dish is always welcome in our house and can be reheated gently from frozen on the hob (never in the slow cooker). Make sure it's piping hot before serving with freshly cooked pasta.

3

Spicy dishes
and curries

Spicy Middle Eastern fish stew

PREPARATION TIME: 10 MINUTES
COOKING TIME: 4–5 HOURS
SERVES 4-6

This aromatic stew is quick to prepare and then the slow cooker does the rest.

1 red onion, peeled and cut into 1cm (½in) pieces

1 green pepper, deseeded and cut into 1cm (½in) pieces

2 tbsp olive oil, plus extra for oiling

1 garlic clove, peeled and finely sliced

1 x 400g (14oz) tin chopped tomatoes

A pinch of saffron strands (optional)

2–3 tsp harissa paste, or to taste

A large pinch of dried oregano

100ml (3½fl oz) dry white wine

1kg (2lb 4oz) firm white skinned fish fillets, such as haddock or pollack, cut into 4cm (1½in) chunks

500g (1lb 2oz) red snapper fillets, skin on and cut into 4cm (1½in) chunks

4 tbsp finely chopped fresh flat-leaf parsley

Sea salt and freshly ground black pepper

Place the vegetables in the slow cooker dish. Add the olive oil, garlic, tomatoes, saffron (if using), harissa, oregano and wine and mix well. Arrange the fish on top in an even layer. Press a piece of lightly oiled parchment paper onto the fish and push down on it gently (this will stop it from drying out). Cover with the lid and cook on low for 4–5 hours or until the fish is opaque.

Spoon the fish onto warm plates. Mix the parsley into the sauce and season to taste with salt and pepper. Spoon over the fish and serve with freshly cooked rice or couscous.

I ALSO LIKE...
to swap the fish for chicken in this recipe. Cook on low for 4–6 hours or until there is no pink meat.

Sea bass with green chilli and coriander

PREPARATION TIME: 15 MINUTES
COOKING TIME: 2–3 HOURS
SERVES 2

I love the sweet, salty, sour combination of flavours in this Southeast Asian dish.

1 large sea bass, about 600–800g (1lb 5oz–1lb 12oz) or to fit in your slow cooker dish without bending, cleaned and gutted

2.5cm (1in) piece fresh root ginger, peeled and roughly chopped

5 garlic cloves, peeled and roughly chopped

1 lemongrass stalk, trimmed and roughly chopped

2 tbsp vegetable oil, plus extra for oiling

1 large green chilli, deseeded and finely chopped

25g (1oz) fresh coriander sprigs, roughly chopped

2 tbsp lime juice

½ tsp sea salt

4 tbsp cold water, plus a little extra if necessary

Place a large piece of parchment paper in the slow cooker dish, pushing it down into the edges, but ensuring that there is plenty of paper hanging over the sides. Wash the fish under cold running water and pat dry with kitchen paper.

Place the ginger, garlic, lemongrass, vegetable oil, chilli, coriander, lime juice, salt and 2 tablespoons of the water into a food processor or mortar and blitz to make a smooth paste, adding a little more water if the paste is very thick.

Spread a little of the green paste over the parchment base in the slow cooker dish and drizzle over the remaining 2 tablespoons of water. Smother the fish inside and out with the rest of the green paste and place it into the dish. Fold the overhanging parchment over the fish and press down around the edges to make a spacious layer around the fish. Cover with the lid and cook on low for 2–3 hours or until the fish is tender and cooked through.

Unwrap the parchment ends and use these as handles to carefully lift the fish out of the slow cooker dish. Place on a warm platter and serve with freshly cooked plain rice.

Fragrant chicken pastilla

PREPARATION TIME: 20 MINUTES
COOKING TIME: 7 HOURS
SERVES 6

Traditionally this is a chicken pie made with fragrant spices and topped with crispy filo pastry. Here the aromatic, slow-cooked filling is wrapped in filo pastry and baked in the oven.

1 medium chicken
1 onion, peeled and coarsely
  grated
½ tsp ground ginger
A large pinch of saffron strands
  (optional)
½ tsp ground cinnamon, plus
  extra for the pastry

½ tsp mixed spice
3 tbsp finely chopped fresh
  flat-leaf parsley
2 tbsp cold water
Sea salt and freshly ground black
  pepper
50g (2oz) butter, melted
16 large sheets filo pastry

Using a large, sharp knife, cut through the chicken, including the bones, to divide the bird into quarters. Wash the chicken under cold running water and pat dry with kitchen paper.

Place the chicken in the slow cooker dish together with the onion, ginger, saffron, cinnamon, mixed spice and parsley. Add the water, cover with the lid and cook on low for 6 hours or until the chicken is tender and there is no pink meat. Remove the chicken from the slow cooker, place on a plate and leave to cool. When it is cool enough to handle remove and discard any skin and bones. Pull the meat into bite-sized pieces.

Skim off and discard any excess fat from the surface of the cooking liquid. Mix the chicken into the flavoured onions and season to taste with salt and pepper. Leave to cool.

Preheat the oven to 170°C (325°F), Gas mark 3. Place a sheet of filo pastry onto a non-stick baking sheet. Brush with a little melted butter and top with another sheet. Repeat to use half of the filo sheets. Top with the cooled chicken mixture, leaving a 2-3cm (¾-1¼in) border around the edge. Top with the remaining filo pastry, brushing butter over each sheet between the layers. Brush the edges with butter and roll up to seal. Sprinkle a little extra cinnamon over the top, if you wish.

Bake in the oven for 40 minutes, then increase the oven temperature to 200°C (400°F), Gas mark 6, and bake for a further 10-15 minutes or until golden.

Tomato buttered chicken

PREPARATION TIME: 10 MINUTES
COOKING TIME: 6–8 HOURS
SERVES 4

**This is not a low-calorie curry option, but it tastes gorgeous and we
all need a treat every now and again!**

4 chicken legs, skin removed
1 onion, peeled and finely sliced
3 garlic cloves, peeled and finely
   sliced
2.5cm (1in) piece fresh root
   ginger, peeled and grated
Seeds from 8 cardamon pods
1 tsp medium curry powder
¼ tsp dried chilli flakes
50g (2oz) butter
2 tomatoes, deseeded and
   chopped

3 tbsp concentrated tomato
   purée
200g (7oz) packet coconut cream
150g (9oz) full-fat Greek yogurt
3 tbsp double cream
1–2 tbsp muscovado sugar, or to
   taste
2 tsp garam masala
Sea salt

Rinse the chicken legs under cold running water and pat dry with kitchen paper. Scatter
the onion over the base of the slow cooker dish, add the garlic, ginger, cardamom
seeds, curry powder, chilli flakes, butter, tomatoes, tomato purée and coconut cream
and mix well. Push the chicken into the curry sauce. Cover with the lid and cook on low
for 6–8 hours or until the chicken is tender and there is no more pink meat.

Carefully remove the chicken from the slow cooker dish, place on a warm platter or
serving dish and cover with a tent of foil. Stir the remaining ingredients into the curry
sauce in the slow cooker dish and season to taste with sea salt. Cover again and leave
for 5–10 minutes to warm through slightly (the resting chicken will be all the better
for it).

Spoon the sauce over the chicken and serve with tzatziki and freshly cooked rice.

FAB FOR THE FREEZER
Leave to cool completely before dividing into portions and freezing. Defrost thoroughly
before reheating gently on the hob (never in the slow cooker).

Easy chicken korma

PREPARATION TIME: 20 MINUTES, PLUS MARINATING (OPTIONAL)
COOKING TIME: 6 HOURS
SERVES 4

Chicken korma has become a family favourite. Here is a very easy version, perfect for a mid-week meal. If you prefer your curry to be hotter then use a stronger curry paste or simply use more of the korma paste!

8 chicken thighs on the bone, skin removed

400g (14oz) full-fat Greek yogurt

6 tbsp good-quality korma curry paste, or to taste

6 tbsp good-quality mango chutney

1 onion, peeled, halved and thinly sliced

1 red pepper, deseeded and diced

2 large ripe tomatoes, roughly chopped

2 tbsp water

100g (3½oz) baby spinach leaves

Sea salt and freshly ground black pepper

A handful of fresh coriander leaves

Rinse the chicken thighs under cold running water, remove the skin and pat dry with kitchen paper.

Mix the yogurt, curry paste and mango chutney together in the slow cooker dish. Add the chicken and turn until the chicken is coated. If you have time, cover and place in the fridge for 30–60 minutes to marinate.

Mix the onion, pepper and tomatoes in with the chicken and drizzle over the water. Cover with the lid and cook on low for 6 hours or until the chicken is tender and there is no more pink meat.

Carefully remove the chicken from the slow cooker and place on warm plates or bowls. Add the spinach to the slow cooker dish and mix in until wilted. Season to taste with salt and pepper and sprinkle the coriander leaves over the top. Serve with rice, poppadums and chutneys.

I ALSO LIKE...
to make this with chicken legs or breast on the bone – without the bones the chicken will dry out very quickly.

Chilli-chicken tortillas

PREPARATION TIME: 5 MINUTES
COOKING TIME: 6-8 HOURS
SERVES 4

This simple recipe is great during the week and couldn't be easier to assemble. The tasty chicken is fabulous in tortillas or equally good in tacos or as a topping for nachos.

8 chicken thighs on the bone, skin removed

2 garlic cloves, peeled and thinly sliced

125g (4½oz) good-quality bought (fresh or from a jar) mild tomato salsa, plus extra to serve

1 large green chilli, finely chopped

1 tsp smoked paprika

½ tsp ground cumin

Sea salt and freshly ground black pepper

1 tbsp fresh coriander leaves

4 large flour tortillas or wraps, to serve

Place the chicken thighs, garlic, salsa, chilli, paprika and cumin in the slow cooker dish and season generously with salt and pepper. Cover with the lid and cook on low for 6–8 hours or until the chicken is tender and there is no pink meat.

Remove the chicken from the slow cooker dish and place on a plate or board. Use 2 forks to shred the meat and discard the bones. Moisten the meat with some of the cooking juices. Add the coriander, then taste and add more seasoning if necessary.

To serve, fold a tortilla in half and then in half again. Open the quartered tortilla to make a pocket. Pile the meat into the pocket and top with more salsa. Serve with some grated Cheddar cheese, shredded lettuce and soured cream or your own choice of toppings.

I ALSO LIKE...
tossing this chicken mixture through freshly cooked pasta – not really geographically correct, but it tastes great!

One-pot Moroccan chicken with couscous

PREPARATION TIME: 10 MINUTES
COOKING TIME: 4¼–5¼ HOURS
SERVES 4

This easy recipe tastes fabulous and is just as good for entertaining as it is for a mid-week supper.

Sea salt and freshly ground black pepper

4 chicken legs, skin removed

1 tbsp olive oil

25g (1oz) butter

2 large onions, peeled and finely diced

2 garlic cloves, peeled and crushed

1 tsp ground cinnamon

1 tsp ground ginger

Finely grated zest of 2 oranges

Finely grated zest of 1 lemon (preferably unwaxed)

250g (9oz) couscous

4 tbsp roughly chopped fresh coriander leaves

Season the chicken legs with salt and pepper. Warm the olive oil and butter in a large frying pan. When hot, add the chicken legs and cook for about 5 minutes or until golden on both sides. Arrange the chicken in the slow cooker dish in a single layer and pour any cooking juices over the top. Scatter the diced onions in a layer over the chicken and add the garlic, spices and citrus zest.

Using a small, serrated knife, cut the top and bottom from the citrus fruit, then place them on a board and slice off the peel in downward strips, being careful to remove the pith as well. Holding the citrus fruit over a small bowl to catch any juice, slice between the thin membranes to release the segments. Do this with each orange and the lemon and add the segments to the chicken together with any juice. Cover with the lid and cook on low for 4–5 hours or until the chicken is tender and there is no pink meat.

Thirty minutes before you wish to eat, sprinkle the couscous over the top and cover again. Cook for 30 minutes or until the couscous is tender. Run a fork through the couscous to separate the grains, then spoon onto warm plates and top with the chicken and sauce. Sprinkle the coriander over and serve. Great with a dressed green salad.

Tomato, potato and coconut curry

PREPARATION TIME: 15 MINUTES
COOKING TIME: 3 HOURS
SERVES 6   VEGETARIAN

This easy vegetarian curry is also great as a side dish if you prefer.

5 medium potatoes, peeled and cut into 2cm (¾in) cubes

1 tbsp vegetable oil

6 garlic cloves, peeled and finely chopped

1 red chilli, finely diced (deseed if you like a milder curry)

1 tsp cumin seeds

½ tsp turmeric

2 tsp ground cumin

1 x 400g (14oz) tin chopped tomatoes

2 tbsp concentrated tomato purée

1 tsp sea salt

200ml (7fl oz) packet coconut cream

250ml (9fl oz) water

2 tsp caster sugar, or to taste

1 tsp red wine vinegar, or to taste

Fresh coriander leaves, for sprinkling

Place the potatoes in a bowl and cover with cold water.

Warm a frying pan over a medium heat. When hot, add the vegetable oil, garlic, chilli and cumin seeds. Cook for 1–2 minutes, stirring until softened but not coloured.

Drain the potatoes and place them and the contents of the frying pan into the slow cooker dish. Add the turmeric, ground cumin, tomatoes, tomato purée, salt, coconut cream and water and mix well. Prod all the potatoes in so that they are covered by liquid (this will prevent them from turning brown). Cover with the lid and cook for 3 hours on low or until the potatoes are tender and the sauce has thickened.

Season with the sugar, vinegar and more salt to taste and sprinkle over the coriander leaves. Serve with naan bread.

I ALSO LIKE...
to add some chicken breast on the bone with the potatoes for a meaty version.

Beetroot and cumin curry

PREPARATION TIME: 10 MINUTES
COOKING TIME: 3-4 HOURS
SERVES 6 AS A SIDE DISH   VEGETARIAN

This easy vegetarian 'curry' is more of a vegetable side dish really,
but it looks and tastes great and will stand up on its own as a main
course when served with rice.

800g (1lb 12oz) fresh raw
  beetroot, peeled and cut into
  2cm (¾in) cubes
2 tbsp vegetable oil
3 garlic cloves, peeled and
  crushed
1 tsp cumin seeds
1 tsp fennel seeds
½ tsp dried chilli flakes

½ tsp ground coriander
1 tsp turmeric
1 x 400g (14oz) tin chopped
  tomatoes
1 tbsp concentrated tomato
  purée
1 tsp sea salt
2 tbsp finely chopped fresh
  coriander

Place the beetroot in the slow cooker dish.

Warm the vegetable oil in a large frying pan. When hot, add the garlic, cumin, fennel
and chilli flakes and stir for 30 seconds, then add the ground coriander and turmeric.
Remove from the heat and spoon into the slow cooker dish. Stir in the tomatoes,
tomato purée and salt. Cover with the lid and cook on low for 3–4 hours or until the
beetroot is tender and the sauce has thickened.

Sprinkle over the chopped coriander and serve.

I ALSO LIKE...
to stir a little coconut cream into this curry when it has cooked, as a variation.

Sri Lankan vegetable curry

PREPARATION TIME: 10 MINUTES, PLUS SOAKING
COOKING TIME: 3–4 HOURS
SERVES 4   VEGETARIAN

Here's my Anglo-Sri Lankan veggie curry in honour of my lovely friend Gayathri.

1 tbsp black mustard seeds

250ml (9fl oz) hot vegetable stock

2 tbsp vegetable oil

2 green chillies

2.5cm (1in) piece fresh root ginger, peeled and chopped

1 onion, peeled and chopped

1 tsp cumin seeds

½ tsp black onion seeds

¼ tsp fennel seeds

½ tsp turmeric

2 tsp ground coriander

½ butternut squash, peeled and cut into cubes

200g (7oz) green beans, trimmed and halved

2 large carrots, peeled and cut into cubes

1 red pepper, deseeded and cut into cubes

½ medium cauliflower, cut into florets

200g (7oz) packet coconut cream

¼ tsp sea salt, plus extra to taste

1–2 tbsp muscovado sugar, or to taste

Roughly chopped coriander leaves, for sprinkling

Lime wedges, to serve

Place the mustard seeds in a small bowl and cover with half of the hot stock. Leave to soak for 30 minutes.

Warm the vegetable oil in a large frying pan over a high heat. When hot, add the chillies, ginger, cumin, onion and fennel seeds and cook, stirring constantly, for 2 minutes or until fragrant. Stir in the turmeric and coriander. Place the warmed spices in a blender or mortar together with the mustard seeds and soaking liquid and blitz or pound until smooth.

Spoon into the slow cooker dish together with the prepared vegetables, coconut cream and salt and mix well, adding the remaining stock as you do so. Cover with the lid and cook on low for 3–4 hours or until the vegetables are tender.

Season with the sugar and more salt to taste. Sprinkle over the chopped coriander and serve with lime wedges to squeeze over and plenty of rice.

Green chilli dhal

PREPARATION TIME: 5 MINUTES
COOKING TIME: 4¼–6¼ HOURS
SERVES 4   VEGETARIAN

This recipe is really easy and cheap to make; it also freezes brilliantly so you can make extra and then freeze it in portions for your next curry. This dhal is great as a side dish or hearty enough to have on its own.

1 tbsp vegetable oil
1 onion, peeled and finely diced
2 garlic cloves, peeled and finely chopped
2.5cm (1in) piece fresh root ginger, peeled and grated
1 large green chilli, finely chopped

½ tsp sea salt, plus extra to taste
1 tsp ground cumin
250g (9oz) red lentils, rinsed and drained
500ml (18fl oz) vegetable stock
1–2 tbsp lime juice, or to taste
A small handful of fresh coriander leaves

Warm the vegetable oil in a large frying pan over a medium heat. When hot, add the onion and cook for 5 minutes or until softened but not coloured. Mix in the garlic, ginger, chilli, salt and cumin and cook for a further 5 minutes, stirring frequently, until fragrant.

Spoon the contents of the pan into the slow cooker dish together with the lentils and stock and mix well. Cover with the lid and cook on low for 4–6 hours or until thickened and the lentils are tender and beginning to break down.

Season to taste with lime juice, half of the coriander leaves and some extra salt if needed. Sprinkle over the rest of the coriander leaves and serve with naan bread.

I ALSO LIKE...
to make a more substantial curry by adding chicken or lamb with the lentils.

Thai pumpkin curry

PREPARATION TIME: 10 MINUTES
COOKING TIME: 2¼–3¼ HOURS
SERVES 4   VEGETARIAN

This fragrant Thai curry tastes great with Thai rice and plenty of fresh coriander.

1 orange-fleshed pumpkin or butternut squash, about 1kg (2lb 4oz), peeled, deseeded and cut into 2–3cm (¾–1¼ in) chunks

1 large red onion, peeled and cut into 2–3cm (¾–1¼ in) chunks

1 red pepper, deseeded and cut into 2–3cm (¾–1¼ in) chunks

2–3 tsp Thai red curry paste, or to taste

1 tbsp fresh lime juice

1 tbsp demerara sugar

½ x 400ml (14fl oz) tin coconut milk

4 large handfuls of baby spinach leaves, washed

2 tbsp Thai fish sauce (optional for vegetarians)

2 spring onions, including their green tops, trimmed and finely shredded

Fresh coriander leaves, for sprinkling

Lime wedges, to serve

Place the pumpkin or butternut squash, onion and pepper in the slow cooker dish together with the curry paste, lime juice and sugar and mix well. Cover with the lid and cook on high for 2–3 hours, stirring once during cooking if you can, until tender and beginning to caramelise.

Add the coconut milk and spinach. Cover again and cook for a further 15 minutes or until the spinach has wilted.

Season with the fish sauce to taste (if using). Ladle into warm bowls and sprinkle the spring onion and coriander leaves over the top. Serve with lime wedges to squeeze over and freshly cooked jasmine rice.

I ALSO LIKE...
adding some sliced chicken thigh meat to the pumpkin mixture at the beginning for a meaty curry.

Lamb tagine with fruit and honey

PREPARATION TIME: 10 MINUTES
COOKING TIME: 6-9 HOURS
SERVES 6

This easy lamb tagine is packed with the authentic flavours of Morocco, but uses simple everyday ingredients.

1.2kg (2lb 12oz) lamb, either neck, shoulder, leg or a mixture, cut into 3-4cm (1¼-1½in) chunks
1 onion, peeled and cut into 3-4cm (1¼-1½in) chunks
½ tsp ground ginger
A large pinch of saffron strands
1 tsp ground coriander
½ tsp ground cinnamon
1¼ tsp crushed dried chilli

100ml (3½fl oz) water
100g (3½oz) ready-to-eat dried prunes
100g (3½oz) ready-to-eat dried apricots
1-2 tsp runny honey (or try orange blossom honey), or to taste
Sea salt and freshly ground black pepper

Place the meat and onion in the slow cooker dish together with the spices and mix well to coat, then pour over the water. Cover with the lid and cook on low for 6–8 hours or until the meat is wonderfully tender.

Increase the heat to high. Scatter over the prunes and apricots and fold in carefully to avoid breaking up the meat. Cover again and cook for a further 30–60 minutes or until the fruit is very soft. Season to taste with the honey and salt and pepper. Serve with couscous.

I ALSO LIKE...
to cook a whole lamb leg, shoulder or shanks with the same spice rub, adjusting the cooking times accordingly.

Jamaican lamb curry

PREPARATION TIME: 20 MINUTES
COOKING TIME: 6¼–8¼ HOURS
SERVES 6

I love the warming combinations of spices in Caribbean cooking.
I have used lamb in this fragrant recipe, but goat would be even
more authentic if you can get it.

2 tbsp vegetable oil

800g (1lb 12oz) lamb shoulder, cut
 into 4cm (1½in) chunks

1 large onion, peeled and cut into
 chunks

2 sweet potatoes, peeled and cut
 into chunks

1 red pepper, deseeded and cut
 into chunks

2 green chillies, roughly chopped
 (deseeded if you prefer a milder
 curry)

5cm (2in) piece fresh root ginger,
 peeled and grated

¼ tsp ground nutmeg

1 tsp ground allspice

Juice of 2 limes

2–3 tbsp dark brown muscovado
 sugar, or to taste

15g (½oz) fresh flat-leaf parsley,
 finely chopped

Warm the vegetable oil in a large frying pan over a high heat. When hot, add the lamb
in 2–3 batches and cook until browned all over, spooning the cooked batches into the
slow cooker dish with a slotted spoon.

Return the frying pan to the heat, add the onion and cook for 5 minutes or until starting
to colour. Transfer them to the slow cooker dish, then stir in all the remaining
ingredients, except the parsley. Cover with the lid and cook on low for 6–8 hours or
until the meat and potatoes are tender.

Stir in the parsley and serve with freshly cooked rice or crusty bread.

I ALSO LIKE...
to make this curry with chicken pieces on the bone, cooking them for a maximum of
6 hours.

Rogan josh lamb shanks in dark almond sauce

PREPARATION TIME: 15 MINUTES
COOKING TIME: 10¼ HOURS
SERVES 4

If you like a mellow, medium-spiced curry then this is the one for you!

4 lamb shanks

4 tbsp vegetable oil

10 whole cloves

1 whole dried chilli

10 black peppercorns

10 whole cardamom pods

1 tbsp ground cumin

1 tbsp ground coriander

1 tbsp desiccated coconut

4 tbsp ground almonds

2 garlic cloves, peeled and
   crushed

1 tsp ground ginger

½ tsp turmeric

1/2 tsp sea salt

About 100ml (3½fl oz) cold water

1 x 400g (14oz) tin chopped
   tomatoes

Rinse the lamb shanks under cold running water and pat dry with kitchen paper. Warm three-quarters of the vegetable oil in a large frying pan over a medium heat. When hot, add the cloves, chilli, peppercorns and cardamom pods and cook for about 30 seconds or until they become dark and fragrant. Remove with a slotted spoon and set aside.

Return the pan to the heat, add the lamb and cook for 5–10 minutes or until browned all over. Remove the meat from the pan with tongs and place in the slow cooker dish.

Return the pan to the heat again and reduce the temperature to medium. Add the cumin, coriander, coconut, almonds and garlic, mix well and cook until the mixture turns a dark gold colour. Remove from the heat and add the ginger, turmeric and salt.

Spoon the mixture into a food processor together with the reserved whole spices and the water and blitz until a smooth paste forms. Add to the slow cooker dish together with the tomatoes and stir well to coat the lamb in the sauce. Cover with the lid and cook on low for 10 hours.

Remove the dish from the base and place on a heatproof surface. Skim off any excess fat with a spoon. Place the shanks on warm serving dishes with plenty of sauce spooned over the top and serve with freshly cooked rice.

Mogul lamb with saffron and raisins

PREPARATION TIME: 15 MINUTES
COOKING TIME: 6¼–8¼ HOURS
SERVES 6

I love this fragrant Middle Eastern-inspired dish. It's amazing with lamb, but also works with chicken if you'd rather - cook the chicken on the bone, though, to stop it from drying out.

2 tbsp vegetable oil

1kg (2lb 4oz) lamb neck or
   shoulder, cut into 3-4cm
   (1¼-1½in) pieces

2 onions, peeled and cut into
   cubes

5 garlic cloves, peeled and sliced

5cm (2in) piece fresh root ginger,
   peeled and shredded

A large pinch of saffron strands

¼ tsp chilli flakes, or to taste

1 tbsp ground coriander

2 tsp ground cumin

½ tsp ground cloves

½ tsp ground cinnamon

2 tbsp seedless raisins

Sea salt and freshly ground black
   pepper

2 tbsp finely chopped fresh flat-
   leaf parsley

Warm the vegetable oil in a large frying pan over a high heat. When hot, add the meat, in batches if necessary, and cook for about 5–10 minutes or until well browned. Transfer the meat to the slow cooker dish with a slotted spoon.

Add all the remaining ingredients except the raisins, seasoning and parsley to the slow cooker dish and mix to combine. Cover with the lid and cook on low for 6–8 hours or until the meat is wonderfully tender.

Remove the slow cooker dish from the base and place on a heatproof surface. Scatter the raisins over the lamb and cover again with the lid. Leave to rest for 10 minutes.

Season with salt and pepper and add the parsley, then mix very gently, being careful not to break up the meat. Serve with couscous or rice.

I ALSO LIKE…

making this recipe with a whole bone-in shoulder of lamb. Cook for at least 8 hours or for up to 12 hours until the meat is falling off the bone.

Indonesian pork

PREPARATION TIME: 20 MINUTES
COOKING TIME: 6-8 HOURS
SERVES 6

Kecap manis is a dark, thick, sweet soy sauce and is available from Asian supermarkets.

850g (1lb 14oz) pork shoulder or leg
4 tomatoes, cut into 1cm (½in) pieces
1 red pepper, deseeded and cut into 1cm (½in) pieces
25g (1oz) desiccated coconut
1 tbsp demerara sugar
Fish sauce, or to taste
Lime juice, or to taste
Lime wedges, to serve

FOR THE PASTE:
1 red chilli, deseeded (if you prefer a milder curry)
1 small onion, peeled and cut into chunks
4 garlic cloves, peeled
1 lemongrass stalk, trimmed and roughly chopped
About 5cm (2in) piece fresh root ginger
1 tbsp dark soy sauce or kecap manis
75g (3oz) desiccated coconut

Rinse the pork under cold running water and pat dry with kitchen paper. Cut the meat into 3-4cm (1¼-1½in) cubes and place in the slow cooker dish together with the tomatoes and pepper.

Place all the paste ingredients in a food processor and blend to make a smooth paste, adding a dash of cold water to loosen it. Mix the paste with the meat, add the remaining desiccated coconut and the sugar and mix until everything is evenly coated.

Cover with the lid and cook on low for 6-8 hours or until the meat is wonderfully tender. Season with a little fish sauce and lime juice to taste, and serve with lime wedges to squeeze over just before eating.

FAB FOR THE FREEZER
This recipe freezes really well for up to three months. Make sure you defrost it thoroughly before gently reheating on the hob (never in the slow cooker).

Easy beef biryani

Preparation time: 10 MINUTES
Cooking time: 3¼–4¼ HOURS
Serves 4

I love biriyanis, and this version is seriously easy and perfect for all the family.

1 tbsp vegetable oil

600g (1lb 5oz) stewing or braising
   steak, cut into 1–2cm (½–¾in)
   pieces

150g (5oz) basmati rice, rinsed
   and drained

150g (5oz) red lentils, rinsed and
   drained

2 tomatoes, chopped

1 x 425g jar good-quality balti
   curry sauce

4 tbsp good-quality mango
   chutney

A small handful of fresh
   coriander leaves, to serve

Warm the vegetable oil in a large frying pan over a high heat. When hot, add the meat and cook for 5–10 minutes or until well browned all over.

Place the meat in the slow cooker dish together with the rice, lentils, tomatoes and curry sauce. Half fill the jar with cold water and rinse out into the slow cooker dish. Cover with the lid and cook on low for 3–4 hours or until both the meat and rice are tender.

Stir the mango chutney gently through the mixture, trying to avoid breaking up the meat, and sprinkle coriander over the top before serving with raita and naan bread.

I ALSO LIKE...
to use 600g (1lb 5oz) beef mince instead of braising steak in this recipe.

Beef with whole spices

PREPARATION TIME: 15 MINUTES
COOKING TIME: 4¼–6¼ HOURS
SERVES 4-6

Don't be put off by the long list of ingredients; this is the easiest dish to make, and tastes SO good.

1kg (2lb 4oz) thick-cut feather
   steak slices or braising steak
   slices
1 large onion, peeled and finely
   sliced
6 tbsp vegetable oil
1 cinnamon stick
10 whole black peppercorns
15 whole cloves
15 whole cardamom pods

2 star anise
2 bay leaves
1 whole dried chilli
2cm (¾in) piece fresh root ginger,
   peeled and shredded
½ tsp sea salt
250ml (9fl oz) hot beef stock
2 tsp garam masala
Sliced green chilli, for sprinkling

Rinse the meat under cold running water and pat dry with kitchen paper. Arrange the onion in a single layer over the base of the slow cooker dish.

Warm the vegetable oil in a large, deep, heavy-based frying pan over a medium heat. When very hot, add the whole spices and cook for about 1 minute or until just coloured and fragrant. Add the beef, in batches if necessary, and cook for about 5 minutes or until browned all over. Add the ginger and salt and mix well, then spoon the contents of the pan, including the oil, into the slow cooker dish. Pour over the stock. Cover with the lid and cook on low for 4–6 hours or until tender.

Remove the beef and spices with a slotted spoon and place in a serving dish. Sprinkle the garam masala and chilli slices over the top. Serve with rice, thick natural yoghurt and naan bread.

COOKING CONVENTIONALLY?
Cook in an ovenproof casserole dish with a tight-fitting lid in an oven preheated to 150°C (300°F), Gas mark 2, for 2–3 hours or until tender.

4

Braises and stews

Summer sausage braise

PREPARATION TIME: 15 MINUTES
COOKING TIME: 6¼–8¼ HOURS
SERVES 6

This braise is great family food and ideal for an easy, economical mid-week supper.

1 tbsp olive oil
12 good-quality pork and herb
  sausages
12 baby shallots, peeled
200g (7oz) smoked streaky bacon,
  diced
2 celery sticks, trimmed and
  chopped

2 garlic cloves, peeled and
  crushed
500g (1lb 2oz) cherry tomatoes
100ml (3½fl oz) dry white wine
100ml (3½fl oz) vegetable stock
Sea salt and freshly ground black
  pepper
25g (1oz) fresh basil

Warm the olive oil in a large frying pan over a medium heat. When hot, add the sausages and cook for 5–10 minutes or until browned. Spoon them into the slow cooker dish.

Return the pan to the heat and add the shallots and bacon and cook for 5 minutes or until golden. Add them to the sausages in the slow cooker.

Mix in the celery, garlic, tomatoes, wine and stock. Cover with the lid and cook on low for 6 hours or until the sauce is thick.

Season to taste with salt and pepper. Rip the basil and scatter it over the sausages. Serve with crusty bread and salad.

FAB FOR THE FREEZER
Leave to cool thoroughly, then place in an airtight plastic container and keep in the freezer for up to three months. Defrost fully before reheating gently on the hob (never in the slow cooker).

Paprika chicken with chorizo

PREPARATION TIME: 15 MINUTES
COOKING TIME: 4½–6½ HOURS
SERVES 4

This is one of my favourite recipes in this book – it's so easy to make and packed with flavour.

1 medium chicken, cut into
  8 pieces on the bone
1–2 tsp smoked paprika
Sea salt and freshly ground black
  pepper
1 tbsp olive oil
100g (3½oz) chorizo, cut into
  chunks
1 onion, peeled and cut into
  chunks

1 red pepper, deseeded and cut
  into chunks
1 green pepper, deseeded and cut
  into chunks
4 garlic cloves, peeled and finely
  sliced
200ml (7fl oz) chicken stock
1 x 400g (14oz) tin chopped
  tomatoes
2 tbsp concentrated tomato purée
2 tbsp soured cream

Wash the chicken pieces under cold running water and pat dry with kitchen paper. Place the paprika and some salt and pepper in a large freezer bag. Add the chicken, seal the top and shake to coat the chicken in the powder.

Warm the olive oil in a large frying pan over a high heat. When hot, add the chorizo and cook for about a minute or until the orangey oil is released. Remove with a slotted spoon and place in the slow cooker dish. Return the pan to the heat, add the chicken together with any remaining paprika and cook for 5–10 minutes or until golden all over. Remove with a slotted spoon and transfer to the slow cooker.

Return the pan to the heat once again and add the onion, peppers and garlic. Stir-fry for about 5 minutes or until softened. Tip into the slow cooker together with any oil in the pan and mix well.

Pour over the stock, tomatoes and tomato purée. Cover with the lid and cook on low for 4–6 hours or until the chicken is tender and there is no pink meat.

Remove the slow cooker dish from the heat and add the soured cream. Leave it to melt into the sauce before serving. Great with chunky bread and a dressed green salad.

Spring chicken and vegetable casserole

PREPARATION TIME: 15 MINUTES
COOKING TIME: 4¼–6¼ HOURS
SERVES 4

Your slow cooker needn't be put away as soon as winter ends. This yummy spring casserole is enough encouragement to keep it cooking throughout the year.

2 tbsp olive oil
4 chicken legs
Sea salt and freshly ground black pepper
12–16 shallots, halved and peeled
2 small fennel bulbs, trimmed and cut into wedges
150g (5oz) baby new potatoes, washed
200g (7oz) baby carrots, washed and halved lengthways

2 bay leaves
4 fresh thyme sprigs
1 tbsp concentrated tomato purée
500ml (18fl oz) dry cider or apple juice
150–200g (5–7oz) baby spinach leaves

Warm the olive oil in a large frying pan over a high heat. Season the chicken legs with salt and pepper, then cook skin side down until golden. Transfer the chicken to the slow cooker dish with a slotted spoon.

Return the frying pan to the heat. Add the shallots and fry for 3–5 minutes or until golden. Add to the slow cooker together with the fennel, potatoes, carrots, bay leaves, thyme and tomato purée and mix well.

Pour over the cider or apple juice. Cover with the lid and cook on low for 4–6 hours or until the chicken is tender and there is no pink meat.

Just before serving stir in the spinach and some extra seasoning to taste. Spoon into deep plates or bowls and serve with mash or crusty bread.

Aromatic chicken with lemon

PREPARATION TIME: 20 MINUTES
COOKING TIME: 6¼–8¼ HOURS
SERVES 4

This simple dish is wonderfully tasty, and equally at home for the family during the week or for guests when entertaining.

Sea salt and freshly ground black pepper
8 mixed chicken pieces on the bone, such as legs, thighs and drumsticks, or joint a whole chicken
1 tbsp olive oil
25g (1oz) butter
2 large onions, peeled and finely sliced

2 garlic cloves, peeled and crushed
1 tsp ground cinnamon
1 tsp ground ginger
2 lemons (preferably unwaxed)
About 150ml (5fl oz) cold water
2 tbsp roughly chopped fresh flat-leaf parsley

Season the chicken pieces with salt and pepper. Warm the olive oil and butter in a large frying pan over a high heat. When hot, add the chicken and cook for about 5 minutes or until golden on both sides.

Place the onions in the slow cooker dish together with the garlic and spices. Arrange the chicken in a single layer over the top and pour over any cooking juices. Finely grate the lemon zest over the chicken and squeeze over the juice, then pour in enough of the water to come halfway up the sides of the chicken. Cover with the lid and cook on low for 6–8 hours or until the chicken is tender and the sauce has thickened.

Sprinkle over the parsley and serve with couscous, rice or mash.

FAB FOR THE FREEZER
Leave the chicken to cool completely before spooning into airtight containers and freezing for up to three months. Defrost thoroughly before reheating gently on the hob (never in the slow cooker).

Country chicken with leeks, cream and bacon

PREPARATION TIME: 15-20 MINUTES
COOKING TIME: 6½ HOURS
SERVES 4-6

The combination of chicken with cream, bacon, tarragon and leeks is just about perfect, and this recipe is no exception.

1 whole medium chicken, cut into 8 pieces, such as drumsticks, thighs and each breast cut in half on the bone
Sea salt and freshly ground black pepper
25g (1oz) butter
1 tbsp olive oil
50g (2oz) plain flour

25g (1oz) smoked streaky bacon, diced
1 tbsp fresh tarragon leaves
450g (1lb) thin leeks, trimmed and cut into 3cm (1¼in) lengths
200ml (7fl oz) dry cider or apple juice
150ml (5fl oz) crème fraîche

Rinse the chicken under cold running water and pat dry with kitchen paper. Season the chicken with salt and pepper.

Warm the butter and olive oil in a large frying pan over a high heat. When hot, add half the chicken pieces, skin side down, and cook for 5–10 minutes, until golden. Transfer the chicken pieces to the slow cooker dish. Repeat this process with the remaining chicken. When all the chicken is browned, and in the slow cooker dish, sprinkle over the flour and mix well until all the pieces are evenly coated.

Return the pan to the heat and add the bacon. Cook for 5 minutes or until just golden. Scatter the bacon and any cooking juices over the chicken together with the tarragon.

Rinse the leeks under cold running water. Drain well and arrange them in a layer over the chicken. Pour over the cider or apple juice. Cover with the lid and cook on low for 6 hours or until the chicken is tender and there is no pink meat.

Add the crème fraîche and gently stir into the sauce, being careful not to break up the chicken pieces. Serve with rice or mash and plenty of seasonal green vegetables.

Sweet and soy ginger chicken

PREPARATION TIME: 10 MINUTES
COOKING TIME: 6 HOURS
SERVES 4

Everyone seems to love this chicken dish – and as a bonus it's really easy and cheap to make too!

75ml (2½fl oz) light soy sauce

2 tbsp dark brown muscovado sugar

4 garlic cloves, peeled and thinly sliced

A large handful of fresh coriander, finely chopped, plus extra leaves to serve

5cm (2in) piece fresh root ginger, peeled and cut into thin strips

1 tbsp cornflour

4 spring onions, trimmed and finely sliced on the diagonal

1 tbsp sherry vinegar, rice wine or white wine vinegar

1 tsp ground coriander

8 chicken drumsticks

Mix the soy sauce, sugar, garlic, chopped coriander, ginger, cornflour, half of the spring onions, the vinegar and ground coriander together in the slow cooker dish.

Add the chicken and mix well to coat in the soy mixture. Cover with the lid and cook on low for about 6 hours or until the chicken is tender and there is no pink meat.

Skim off and discard any fat from the surface of the cooking liquid. Scatter the remaining spring onions and some coriander leaves over the chicken before serving with freshly cooked rice.

I ALSO LIKE...
making this recipe with pork spareribs.

Winter vegetable stew with thyme dumplings

PREPARATION TIME: 10 MINUTES

COOKING TIME: 4–6 HOURS

SERVES 4   VEGETARIAN

Vegetarians seem to miss out on hearty stew-like fare, which is often monopolised by gutsy meat dishes. This recipe ticks all the hearty, warming, comfort food boxes that you'd expect from the best of winter stews. Make sure your slow cooker dish can be used in the oven before making this recipe.

2 large waxy potatoes, peeled and cut into chunks

2 tbsp plain flour

1 onion, peeled and cut into chunks

1 leek, trimmed and cut into chunks

3 carrots, peeled and cut into chunks

2 celery sticks, trimmed and cut into chunks

75g (3oz) pearl barley

2 fresh thyme sprigs

250ml (9fl oz) dry cider or apple juice

250ml (9fl oz) hot vegetable stock or water

Sea salt and freshly ground black pepper

FOR THE THYME DUMPLINGS:

150g (5oz) self-raising flour

75g (3oz) vegetable suet

1 tbsp fresh thyme leaves

About 100ml (4fl oz) cold water

Place the potatoes in the slow cooker dish and mix with the flour. Scatter the vegetables and pearl barley into the slow cooker so that they completely cover the potato (if the potato is in contact with the air it will turn brown). Add the thyme and pour over the cider or apple juice and stock (it should just cover the vegetables). Cover with the lid and cook on low for 4–6 hours or until the vegetables are tender and the sauce is thickened.

Mix the stew and season to taste with salt and pepper. At this point, make the dumplings (check that your slow cooker dish can be used in the oven first).

Preheat the oven to 200°C (400°F), Gas mark 6. Mix the flour, suet and thyme together in a large bowl and season to taste. Add enough water to form a firm dough. Drop 8 large spoonfuls of the dough into the hot stew, pushing them in so they are only just poking out.

Place the slow cooker dish in the oven and cook, uncovered, for 20 minutes or until the dumplings are golden and cooked through. Serve with seasonal greens and mash.

I ALSO LIKE...
to make a meaty chicken version of this stew. Brown some chicken pieces in a hot frying pan with a little olive or vegetable oil until just golden, then add them to the slow cooker with the vegetables and barley at the beginning.

Fruity Moroccan lamb shanks

PREPARATION TIME: 10 MINUTES
COOKING TIME: 8 HOURS
SERVES 4

Lamb shanks are perfect for slow cooking. Their central bone keeps the meat tender and moist and the long slow cooking helps to break down the fat and the muscle, leaving the meat meltingly tender. They go wonderfully with fruity sauces, and this one is no exception.

4 lamb shanks

1 x 400g (14oz) tin chopped tomatoes

2 tbsp concentrated tomato purée

2 tbsp chunky apricot jam

4 garlic cloves, peeled and roughly chopped

Finely grated zest and juice of 1 orange

½ tsp ground ginger

½ tsp ground cinnamon

1 fresh rosemary sprig

600g (1lb 5oz) baby new potatoes, washed

Sea salt and freshly ground black pepper

Rinse the lamb shanks under cold running water and pat dry with kitchen paper. Mix the tomatoes, tomato purée, jam, garlic, orange zest and juice, ginger, cinnamon and rosemary together in the slow cooker dish. Add the potatoes and lamb and mix well to coat. Pull the lamb to the surface, allowing the potatoes to fall beneath, and season the lamb well with salt and pepper. Cover with the lid and cook on low for 8 hours or until the meat and potatoes and tender.

Season again to taste before serving with seasonal greens.

I ALSO LIKE...
to use a handful of dried apricots, or when in season fresh stoned apricots if I have them. They will make the sauce thicker, though, so add a little water if you prefer.

Barnsley hotpot

PREPARATION TIME: 10 MINUTES
COOKING TIME: 4–5 HOURS
SERVES 4

I'm a real fan of Lancashire hotpot. Here I'm using Barnsley chops, which are best described as a double lamb chop, cut across the loin with the bone running through the centre. They are now available in most decent supermarkets, or ask your butcher to prepare some for you.

4 Barnsley chops

25g (1oz) butter

3 large baking potatoes, peeled and cut into 5mm (¼in) slices

2 small onions, peeled and finely sliced

1 large carrot, peeled and sliced

2 garlic cloves, peeled and crushed

3 tbsp plain flour

1 tsp fresh thyme leaves

Sea salt and freshly ground black pepper

300ml (10fl oz) hot lamb or chicken stock

1 tbsp Worcestershire sauce

Rinse the chops under cold running water and pat dry with kitchen paper. Butter the inside of the slow cooker dish liberally. Arrange the potato slices in an overlapping layer over the base of the dish. Top with the onions, carrot and garlic.

Place the flour and thyme leaves in a large freezer bag and season with salt and pepper. Add the lamb, seal the top and shake to coat in the flour. Tip the meat and any excess flour over the vegetables.

Mix the hot stock and Worcestershire sauce together in a jug, then pour the mixture over the meat. Cover with the lid and cook for 4–5 hours on low or until the meat is tender. Place the chops on warm plates and spoon over the vegetables to serve.

I ALSO LIKE...
using cubed lamb shoulder or neck instead of the chops in this recipe – you'll need about 500–600g (1lb 2oz–1lb 5oz).

Orange braised lamb

PREPARATION TIME: 10 MINUTES
COOKING TIME: 6½-8½ HOURS
SERVES 4

The rounded citrus flavour of the orange works really well to cut through the richness of the lamb in this dish.

600g (1lb 5oz) lamb neck fillet

2 tbsp olive oil

1 carrot, peeled and finely diced

2 celery sticks, trimmed and
   finely diced

100ml (3½fl oz) white wine

2 bay leaves, broken

2 fresh rosemary sprigs

2 garlic cloves, peeled and finely
   chopped

2 oranges

1 tbsp concentrated tomato purée

200ml (7fl oz) lamb or vegetable
   stock

Sea salt and freshly ground black
   pepper

Wash the lamb under cold running water and pat dry on kitchen paper. Warm half of the olive oil in a large frying pan over a high heat. When hot, add the carrot and celery and cook for 5 minutes or until softened but not coloured. Using a slotted spoon transfer to the slow cooker dish. Return the pan to the heat and add the remaining oil. When hot, add the lamb and cook for 5–10 minutes or until browned all over (do this in batches). Transfer the meat to the slow cooker with a slotted spoon.

Return the pan to the heat again and add the wine. Stir vigorously to scrape up any bits from the bottom of the pan, then add to the meat together with the bay leaves, rosemary and garlic.

Finely grate the zest of the oranges and place all but about 2 teaspoons of the zest in the slow cooker. Add the juice of 1½ oranges and reserve the extra zest and juice from the remaining orange half. Add the tomato purée and stock to the slow cooker and stir together well. Cover with the lid and cook on low for 6–8 hours or until the meat is tender.

Skim off any fat from the surface of the liquid. Remove the meat with a slotted spoon and keep warm. Strain the sauce through a sieve into a clean saucepan. Bring to the boil and bubble for 5–10 minutes or until reduced by half. Remove from the heat, add the reserved zest and juice and season to taste. Serve the meat with the sauce spooned over.

Aromatic Asian pork with noodles

PREPARATION TIME: 15 MINUTES
COOKING TIME: 6¼–8¼ HOURS
SERVES 6

This recipe is so tasty. You will need to vary the amount of stock depending on the size of your slow cooker.

1.5kg (3lb 5oz) pork belly, cut into 4cm (1½in) chunks

1.5 litres (2½ pints) hot pork or chicken stock, or enough to cover the meat

7 spring onions, trimmed

100ml (3½fl oz) light soy sauce

100ml (3½fl oz) sherry

5cm (2in) piece fresh ginger root, peeled and finely sliced

1 tsp Chinese five spice powder

1–2 red chillies, sliced (and deseeded if you prefer a less spicy dish)

2 tbsp dark brown muscovado sugar

Place the pork in a large saucepan and pour over enough boiling water to cover. Bring to the boil over a high heat, then reduce the heat and simmer for 5 minutes. Skim off and discard any scum that forms on the surface. Drain the meat thoroughly in a colander.

Place the pork in the slow cooker dish and pour over enough hot stock to cover the meat. Cut 6 of the spring onions into chunks and add them to the slow cooker together with all the remaining ingredients and stir well. Cover with the lid and cook on low for 6–8 hours or until the meat is tender.

Remove the meat from the liquid with a slotted spoon and set aside in a warm place. Skim off and discard any excess fat from the surface of the cooking liquid. Strain the remaining meaty juices through a sieve into a clean saucepan and bring to the boil over a high heat. Once boiling, leave it to bubble rapidly for 5 minutes, skimming off any fat or scum from the surface as you go, until reduced and syrupy.

Add the reserved pork to the hot sauce and gently fold through until piping hot. Shred the remaining spring onion into thin strips. Serve the pork with noodles or rice, spooning over plenty of sauce and sprinkling with the shredded spring onion.

Lemon and honey pork chops

PREPARATION TIME: 10 MINUTES
COOKING TIME: 4¼–6¼ HOURS
SERVES 6

You might think that the lemon chunks would be overpowering in this recipe, but instead they become caramelised and really make this dish.

1 tbsp olive oil
6 thick-cut, bone-in pork chops
  (with fat)
2 red onions, peeled and finely
  sliced
12 garlic cloves, peeled
2 fresh thyme sprigs, leaves only
1 lemon, cut into chunks

Sea salt and freshly ground black
  pepper
150ml (5fl oz) pork, vegetable or
  chicken stock
125g (4½oz) clear honey
A small handful of fresh oregano
  leaves

Warm the olive oil in a large frying pan over a high heat. When hot, add the chops and cook briefly until browned on each side.

Place the onions in the slow cooker dish and scatter over the garlic and thyme. Top with the chops. Tuck the lemon chunks in between the meat and season with salt and pepper, before drizzling over the stock and the honey. Cover with the lid and cook on low for 4–6 hours or until the pork is tender and the onions are soft.

Season to taste and mix everything together. Scatter the oregano leaves over the top before serving with mash or new potatoes.

I ALSO LIKE...
to cook a pork shoulder roast in the same way, adjusting the cooking time accordingly to about 8 hours on low (depending on weight).

Ham hocks in cola

PREPARATION TIME: 10 MINUTES
COOKING TIME: 6 HOURS 10 MINUTES
SERVES 4

I'm a big fan of ham hocks, so I've been thrilled to see them back in supermarkets and butchers again. This is my nod to a retro recipe idea that has been around for years in America using whole hams. If you don't like the thought of this recipe, I urge you to try it – I think you'll be pleasantly surprised!

2 hocks

2 litres (3½ pints) cola, not diet

1 red onion, peeled and finely sliced

2 bay leaves, broken

2 fresh thyme sprigs, leaves only

Place the hocks in a large saucepan and cover with cold water. Bring to the boil over a high heat and cook for 5 minutes. Drain the hocks in a colander and refresh under cold running water.

Place the onion in the slow cooker dish together with the bay leaves and the thyme leaves. Place the hocks on top and pour over enough cola to just cover them. Cover with the lid and cook on low for 4 hours.

Remove the lid and increase the heat to high. Continue to cook, uncovered for a further 2 hours, basting the hams with the cola every 30 minutes or so, until the sauce has thickened and the hocks are looking shiny and glazed.

Remove the hocks from the slow cooker and place on a board. Using 2 forks, remove and discard (or see below) any substantial pieces of fat, then pull the meat apart into portions. Serve with mash and with the cola sauce spooned over.

I ALSO LIKE...

to indulge by making fattening but gorgeous crispy pork crackling! When the fat is removed from the pork (see above), place it on a baking sheet and cook in a very hot oven preheated to 230°C (450°F), Gas mark 8, for 5–7 minutes or until bubbling and crisp. Remove from the oven and leave for cool for 5 minutes before cutting into pieces with a sharp knife.

Pig cheeks in cider

PREPARATION TIME: 10 MINUTES
COOKING TIME: 8 HOURS
SERVES 4

I love pig cheeks when I go out to a restaurant, and fortunately now most decent supermarkets and butchers have made them available to home cooks too. Do try them – their flavour and texture are gloriously rich. Here they are cooked in a gorgeous, creamy cider sauce.

8 pig cheeks
2 tbsp plain flour
Sea salt and freshly ground black pepper
500ml (18fl oz) dry cider or apple juice

1 celery stick, trimmed and diced
1 onion, peeled and finely sliced
3 tbsp cider vinegar
3-4 fresh thyme sprigs
2 tbsp crème fraîche

Rinse the cheeks under cold running water and pat dry with kitchen paper. Place the flour into a large freezer bag and season with salt and pepper. Add the pork, seal the top and shake in the bag to coat in the flour.

Place the cheeks and any excess flour in the slow cooker dish. Add the cider or apple juice, celery, onion, vinegar and thyme, and mix well. Cover with the lid and cook on low for 8 hours or until the meat is tender and the sauce has thickened.

Remove the cheeks with a slotted spoon and place on warm plates. Stir the crème fraîche into the sauce and season to taste before spooning over the pork. This dish just has to be eaten with mash!

I ALSO LIKE...
making this recipe with pork chops on the bone.

Easy beef stew

PREPARATION TIME: 15 MINUTES
COOKING TIME: 8 HOURS
SERVES 6

This comforting stew is, as the title suggests, really easy and quick to make. It doesn't require any browning or complicated preparation – you just throw it all in! It is perfect for an after-work supper or for entertaining when preparation time is limited.

1.5kg (3lb 5oz) stewing or braising steak, cut into 3-4cm (1¼-1½in) chunks

3 tbsp concentrated tomato purée

3 tbsp balsamic vinegar

2 tbsp plain flour

2 onions, peeled and cut into 2-3cm (¾-1¼in) chunks

2 large carrots, peeled and cut into 2-3cm (¾-1¼in) chunks

450g (1lb) baby new potatoes, washed

3 garlic cloves, peeled and crushed

2 bay leaves, broken

Sea salt and freshly ground black pepper

Place the beef in the slow cooker dish together with the tomato purée, vinegar and flour and mix until the beef is well coated.

Add the vegetables, garlic and bay leaves to the slow cooker and mix well. Season with salt and pepper. Cover with the lid and cook on low for 8 hours or until the meat is meltingly tender.

Serve with salad or seasonal vegetables.

FAB FOR THE FREEZER
Make a double batch and freeze in portions for a day when you don't have time to cook. Defrost thoroughly before reheating gently on the hob (never in a slow cooker).

Pastitsada (Greek beef stew)

PREPARATION TIME: 10 MINUTES
COOKING TIME: 6¼–8¼ HOURS
SERVES 4

Traditionally from Corfu, this dish is often made with a whole slow cook joint like brisket. Here, beef mince makes it perfect for a mid-week supper.

2 tbsp olive oil
500g (1lb 2oz) beef mince
1 large onion, peeled and diced
2 large carrots, peeled and diced
1 tsp ground allspice
150ml (5fl oz) red wine
1 x 400g (14oz) tin chopped
  tomatoes with garlic
1 beef stock cube
Sea salt and freshly ground black
  pepper

Warm the olive oil in large pan over a high heat. When hot, add the mince and cook, stirring occasionally to break up the meat, for 5–10 minutes or until well browned. Spoon the mince into the slow cooker dish.

Return the pan to the heat and add the onion. Stir-fry for 2–3 minutes or until just starting to colour. Add to the slow cooker together with the carrots, allspice, wine and tomatoes. Crumble over the stock cube and mix well. Cover with the lid and cook on low for 6–8 hours or until rich and thick.

Season to taste with salt and pepper and serve with rice or creamy mash and seasonal green vegetables.

I ALSO LIKE...
using 500g (1lb 2oz) cubed beef braising steak for this recipe instead.

Beef stroganoff

PREPARATION TIME: 15 MINUTES
COOKING TIME: 8 HOURS
SERVES 4

I love beef stroganoff, but disappointingly the meat is often tough.
In this recipe long slow cooking ensures that the beef is amazingly
tender.

500g (1lb 2oz) beef chuck or
  stewing steak
1 large onion, peeled and finely
  sliced
500g (1lb 2oz) cup mushrooms,
  cleaned and sliced
2 tbsp cornflour

2 tbsp brandy or water
4 tbsp cold water
Sea salt and freshly ground black
  pepper
2 tbsp Dijon mustard
150ml (5fl oz) soured cream
1 tbsp finely chopped fresh dill

Cut the beef, across the grain, into thin strips. Mix the beef, onion, mushrooms,
cornflour and brandy or water together in the slow cooker dish. Add the 4 tablespoons
of water and season well with salt and pepper. Cover with the lid and cook on low for
8 hours or until the meat is tender.

Stir in the mustard, soured cream and the dill and season again to taste. Serve with
freshly cooked rice or long thin pasta or noodles.

COOKING CONVENTIONALLY?
Preheat the oven to 180°C (350°F), Gas mark 4. Use an ovenproof casserole dish with
a tight-fitting lid instead of a slow cooker and add 250ml (9fl oz) cold water in addition
to the brandy or water. Cover and transfer to the oven. Cook for about 2 hours or until
the beef is tender. Stir in the mustard, cream and dill and continue as above.

Beef in black bean sauce

PREPARATION TIME: 20 MINUTES
COOKING TIME: 6¼ HOURS
SERVES 6

This is a cracking recipe – although I say so myself! It's easy to make and the meat is gloriously tender. Buy the vacuum-packed Chinese fermented beans from Asian supermarkets, or buy the sauce in any supermarket.

750g (1lb 10oz) beef braising or stewing steak (chuck works well)
1 tbsp vegetable oil
1 tsp caster sugar
1 tbsp dark soy sauce
1 tbsp Chinese rice wine or dry sherry
1½ tsp cornflour
2 peppers (one green and one red if possible), deseeded and sliced into strips

4 spring onions, trimmed and cut into 3cm (1¼in) lengths
2 garlic cloves, peeled and finely chopped
About 3cm (1¼in) piece fresh root ginger, peeled and finely chopped
25g (1oz) Chinese fermented black beans, finely chopped, or 2 tbsp black bean sauce

Cut the beef, across the grain, into thin strips. Warm the vegetable oil in a large frying pan over a high heat. When hot, add the meat in batches and cook for 5–10 minutes or until browned all over. Transfer to the slow cooker dish, then add the sugar, soy sauce, rice wine or sherry and cornflour. Leave to marinate for 10 minutes.

Add the prepared vegetables and black beans or sauce to the slow cooker and mix well. Cover with the lid and cook on low for 6 hours or until the beef is tender.

Serve with freshly cooked rice or noodles.

I ALSO LIKE...
making this recipe with strips of lamb shoulder or neck.

5

Roasts

Roast chicken with saffron and Moroccan vegetables

PREPARATION TIME: 15 MINUTES
COOKING TIME: 6 HOURS
SERVES 4

The slow cooker makes easy work of a roast chicken and ensures wonderfully moist meat. Harissa is a spicy Moroccan chilli paste and is available from all good supermarkets.

1–1.5kg (2lb 4oz)–3lb 5oz) whole free-range chicken

1 orange

2 red onions, peeled

2 large pinches of saffron strands

2 celery sticks, trimmed and cut into large chunks

1 large carrot, peeled and cut into large chunks

1 large courgette, trimmed and cut into large chunks

2 tsp harissa paste, or to taste

Sea salt and freshly ground black pepper

2 tbsp chopped fresh coriander

Wash the chicken inside and out and pat dry with kitchen paper. Cut the orange in half and push one of the pieces and one of the red onions into the cavity of the chicken.

Warm the juice from the other orange half in a small saucepan over a medium heat for 1 minute. Remove from the heat and add the saffron strands. Leave to stand for 5–10 minutes.

Cut the remaining onion into large chunks and place in the slow cooker dish together with the remaining vegetables. Mix in the harissa paste and season with salt and pepper. Place the chicken on the bed of vegetables.

Using a pastry brush or your fingers, 'paint' the saffron-infused orange juice over the chicken (it will colour it a beautiful yellow). Cover with the lid and cook on low for 6 hours or until the chicken is tender and there is no pink meat.

Remove the chicken from the slow cooker, place on a board and leave to rest for 10–15 minutes. Skim off any excess fat from the surface of the cooking liquid. Stir the coriander and seasoning to taste into the vegetables and serve immediately.

Roast chicken with clementines

PREPARATION TIME: 10 MINUTES
COOKING TIME: 6½ HOURS
SERVES 4

This simple roast chicken recipe works wonders at any time of the year.

1-1.5kg (2lb 4oz-3lb 5oz) whole free-range chicken
2 tbsp olive oil
4 clementines
1 onion, peeled and very finely sliced
2 large carrots, peeled and diced

2 tbsp clear honey
150ml (5fl oz) dry white wine
25g (1oz) butter, cut into cubes
Sea salt and freshly ground black pepper
2 tbsp chopped fresh flat-leaf parsley

Wash the chicken inside and out and pat dry with kitchen paper. Warm the olive oil in a large frying pan over a high heat. When hot, add the chicken and cook for 10 minutes, turning frequently until golden all over. Set aside.

Wash and dry the clementines. Place two of them, skin on, inside the cavity of the chicken. Roughly chop the remaining clementines, again with the skin on, and place them in the slow cooker dish together with the onion, carrots, honey and wine and mix together well.

Place the chicken on the bed of fruit and vegetables and pour over any juices that may have gathered in the pan. Cover with the lid and cook on low for 6 hours or until the chicken is tender and there is no pink meat.

Remove the chicken from the slow cooker, place on a board and leave to rest for 10-15 minutes.

Meanwhile, skim off any excess fat from the surface of the cooking liquid, then strain the sauce through a sieve into a saucepan. Bring to the boil over a high heat and bubble vigorously for 5-10 minutes or until reduced by about one-third. Reduce the heat and slowly whisk in the butter, piece by piece. Season to taste with salt and pepper and add the parsley. Carve the chicken and serve with the sauce.

I ALSO LIKE...
to use other citrus fruits – lemons, blood oranges and tangerines all work well.

Roast turkey leg with red wine sauce

PREPARATION TIME: 20 MINUTES
COOKING TIME: 4¾–6¾ HOURS
SERVES 4

Coq au vin has always been a favourite of mine, but I often use turkey instead of chicken. It's so economical and cooks brilliantly in the slow cooker.

2 turkey drumsticks

50g (2oz) plain flour

Sea salt and freshly ground black pepper

25g (1oz) butter

1 tbsp olive oil

12 baby shallots, peeled

200g (7oz) smoked streaky bacon, diced

250ml (9fl oz) red wine

2 bay leaves, broken

2 fresh thyme sprigs

2 celery sticks, trimmed and diced

4 garlic cloves, peeled and roughly chopped

250ml (9fl oz) chicken stock or water

2 tbsp concentrated tomato purée

Place the turkey in a large freezer bag with the flour and some salt and pepper. Seal the top and shake the bag to coat the meat in the flour.

Warm a large frying pan over a high heat, and when hot add the butter and olive oil. When the butter has melted, add the shallots and fry for 5–10 minutes or until golden. Transfer them to the slow cooker dish with a slotted spoon.

Return the pan to the heat, add the bacon and cook for 3–5 minutes or until golden. Add them to the shallots in the slow cooker. Finally brown the turkey legs in the same pan for 5–10 minutes or until golden all over. Transfer to the slow cooker.

Add the wine to the now empty frying pan and stir well to scrape up any bits from the bottom of the pan. Pour over the turkey and surround with the herbs, celery, garlic, stock and tomato purée. Cover with the lid and cook on low for 4–6 hours or until the turkey is tender and there is no pink meat.

Remove the meat from the slow cooker, place on a plate and set aside. Skim off any excess fat from the surface of the cooking liquid and strain the liquid through a large sieve into a large saucepan. Set the vegetables aside with the turkey.

Bring the sauce to the boil over a high heat and cook for 5–10 minutes or until reduced by about one-third, then season to taste with salt and pepper. When the turkey is just cool enough to handle, remove the meat from the bones and discard any skin. Mix the meat, reserved vegetables and bacon into the sauce. Serve with mash and seasonal green vegetables.

Duck with sticky pomegranate and orange sauce

PREPARATION TIME: 5 MINUTES
COOKING TIME: 3¼–4¼ HOURS
SERVES 4–6

This wonderful dish is great served with couscous.

2–2.5kg (4lb 8oz–5lb 8oz) free-
  range duck
3 large oranges
1 large onion, peeled

3 fresh thyme sprigs
250ml (9fl oz) pomegranate juice
Sea salt and freshly ground black
  pepper

Remove the giblets and any excess fat from the inside of the bird. Prick the skin all over with the tip of a sharp knife, then place the duck in a clean kitchen sink and pour a

Continued overleaf

kettle full of boiling water over the bird (this will help to remove some of the excess fat). Repeat this process again.

Cut one of the oranges in half and use it to fill the cavity of the bird together with the whole onion and thyme. Place the duck, breast side down, in the slow cooker dish, cover with the lid and cook on low for 1 hour.

Carefully pour the fat away into a bowl (don't discard it, though – it's great for crispy roast potatoes). Cover with the lid again and continue cooking the duck for a further hour, then pour the fat off a second time. Turn the bird over, so it is breast side up.

Finely grate the zest from the remaining 2 oranges over the duck, then pour over the orange juice and half of the pomegranate juice. Cover with the lid again and increase the temperature to high. Cook for 1–2 hours or until tender and the juices run clear when tested with the tip of a knife (or see tip below).

Carefully lift the bird out of the slow cooker, draining off any juices that may have gathered in the cavity and place on a plate or board. Cover with a tent of foil and leave to rest in a warm place for about 15 minutes.

Skim off the excess fat in the slow cooker dish, leaving only the meaty cooking juices behind. Pour these juices into a small saucepan together with the remaining pomegranate juice. Season to taste with salt and pepper and bring to the boil over a high heat. Boil for 5–10 minutes or until reduced and thickened slightly. Taste and add more seasoning if necessary, then carve the duck and serve with the sticky sauce spooned over the top.

I ALSO LIKE...
to test poultry and duck with a meat thermometer before serving – poke the clean thermometer into the thickest part of the meat, avoiding the bones as these hold the heat. The core temperature should be at least 75°C (167°F).

Winter vegetable gratin

PREPARATION TIME: 15-20 MINUTES
COOKING TIME: 3-4 HOURS
SERVES 6   VEGETARIAN

This comforting root vegetable gratin tastes fantastic and is just as good on its own as it is as an accompaniment.

25g (1oz) softened butter

3 medium potatoes, peeled

½ small swede, peeled

1 parsnip, peeled

Sea salt and freshly ground black
  pepper

125g (4½oz) extra mature

Cheddar cheese, grated

1 tsp fresh thyme leaves (lemon
  thyme tastes great in this!)

300ml (10fl oz) double cream

300ml (10fl oz) milk

4 medium eggs, beaten

1 garlic clove

Using about a third of the butter, butter the inside of the slow cooker dish generously. Slice the vegetables into very thin 2-3mm (1⁄16-1⁄8in) slices (a mandolin or food processor with slicing attachment is the easiest way to do this).

Arrange the potato slices in an overlapping layer over the base of the dish. Season well with salt and pepper and dot with a little more of the butter. Sprinkle a third of the cheese and a third of the thyme leaves over the top. Repeat this process again using the swede slices first, and then the parsnips. Aim for the dish to be no more than half full.

In a large bowl, whisk the cream, milk and beaten eggs together, then pour the mixture over the vegetables (it should cover the vegetables completely). Cover with the lid and cook on high for 3-4 hours or until the vegetables are tender when tested with the tip of a knife.

Remove the dish from the slow cooker base and leave to rest for about 30 minutes.

If your slow cooker can be used under the grill (check the manufacturer's instructions) preheat the grill to its highest setting. Grill the top of the gratin for 3-5 minutes or until golden before serving. If not, just serve it as it is.

COOKING CONVENTIONALLY?
Layer the ingredients into a large ovenproof dish then cover with a double layer of buttered foil. Cook in an oven preheated to 160°C (325°F), Gas mark 3, for 1 hour before removing the foil and cooking for a further 30 minutes or until tender and golden.

Rolled breast of lamb with redcurrant and rosemary

PREPARATION TIME: 15 MINUTES
COOKING TIME: 4-6 HOURS
SERVES 4

It's great to see lamb breast readily available in supermarkets again. It's a fabulously flavoursome cut, perfect for slow cooking.

2 rolled breasts of lamb, about 400g (14oz) each

175g (6oz) redcurrant jelly

3 fresh rosemary sprigs, roughly chopped

2 garlic cloves, peeled and crushed

2 shallots, peeled and finely chopped

3 tbsp natural breadcrumbs

2 red onions, peeled and finely sliced

100ml (3½fl oz) red wine or water

Snip the string from the lamb and unravel, laying the pieces out flat on a board.

Mix the redcurrant jelly, rosemary, garlic, shallots and breadcrumbs together in a bowl. Spread the redcurrant mixture over the lamb, then top with the other piece of meat. Roll the whole lot up together like a Swiss roll into one cylindrical shape and re-tie with kitchen string.

Place the red onions in the slow cooker dish to make a bed for the meat. Top with the lamb and pour over the wine or water together with any remaining redcurrant stuffing that may have oozed out during rolling. Cover with the lid and cook on low for 4-6 hours or until tender.

Remove the meat from the slow cooker, place on a plate or board and leave to rest for about 5 minutes before carving into 4 thick slices.

COOKING CONVENTIONALLY?
Cook in a roasting tin in an oven preheated to 160°C (325°F), Gas mark 3, for about 1 hour or until tender.

Rolled lamb with capers and anchovies

PREPARATION TIME: 15 MINUTES
COOKING TIME: 6-8 HOURS
SERVES 4

Lamb and anchovies are a surprising but brilliant team. The saltiness of the fish really lifts the flavour of the meat.

1-1.5kg (2lb 4oz-3lb 5oz) rolled shoulder of lamb, bone removed

2 tbsp baby capers in brine, rinsed and drained

2 garlic cloves, peeled

1 x 50g (2oz) tin anchovy fillets in olive oil, drained

2 fresh lemon thyme sprigs, leaves only

2 tbsp cold water

Remove the strings from the lamb and unroll. Place it fat side down on a board.

Place the capers, garlic, anchovies and thyme leaves into a mini processor or use a pestle and mortar and blitz or pound to make a coarse paste. Spread the paste over the meat side of the lamb. Re-roll the lamb to form its original shape and tie with kitchen string at 2cm (¾in) intervals.

Place the meat in the slow cooker dish and drizzle over the water. Cover with the lid and cook on low for 6-8 hours or until tender.

Remove the lamb from the slow cooker, place on a board and leave to rest for 10 minutes before carving into thick slices, discarding the string. Serve with roasted new potatoes and dollops of Greek yoghurt.

I ALSO LIKE...
to omit the anchovies in this recipe when any fish-hating friends come for supper! The recipe still tastes great; just add 2 tablespoons of olive oil to the paste when you make it.

Gammon with Cumberland and orange sauce

PREPARATION TIME: 10 MINUTES
COOKING TIME: 6-8 HOURS
SERVES 6

Gammon with Cumberland sauce and mashed potatoes reminds me of Boxing Day with all the family. It is a fabulous combination of flavours and the slow cooker makes easy work of the cooking, as it's an all-in-one dish.

1.5kg (3lb 5oz) gammon joint (check this will fit your slow cooker dish)

1 red onion, peeled and thinly sliced

1 orange

1 lemon (preferably unwaxed)

6 tbsp good-quality redcurrant jelly

4 tbsp port

1 tsp mustard powder

1 tsp ground ginger

Sea salt and freshly ground black pepper

Wash the gammon under cold running water and pat dry with kitchen paper. Place the onion in the slow cooker dish and top with the gammon, fat side up.

Using a potato peeler, thinly pare off the zest from the orange and lemon, then using a sharp knife cut the zest into very thin strips. Place the strips in a small bowl and pour over enough boiling water to cover. Leave to stand for 5 minutes to draw out the bitter-tasting oils. Drain well.

Remove the segments from the orange over a bowl to catch the juice and scatter these with any juice around the gammon. Add the blanched zests, the juice of half a lemon, the redcurrant jelly, port, mustard powder and ginger to the slow cooker. Cover with the lid and cook on low for 6-8 hours or until the meat is tender.

Remove the gammon from the slow cooker, place on a plate or board and leave to rest under a tent of foil for 10 minutes.

Meanwhile, skim off any excess fat from the surface of the cooking liquid. Season the remaining sauce to taste and mix well to ensure that there are no lumps of mustard powder remaining. Serve the gammon in slices with the sauce spooned over.

All-in-one pork and apple sauce

PREPARATION TIME: 15 MINUTES
COOKING TIME: 8-10 HOURS
SERVES 6-8

An absolute favourite in our house – and so easy!

2kg (4lb 7oz) pork belly (check
   that it fits the slow cooker – it
   needs to be just larger than the
   base of the dish)
3 Bramley apples, peeled, cored
   and diced

Finely grated zest and juice of
   1 lemon (preferably unwaxed)
2 tsp caster sugar
1 fresh thyme sprig
2 bay leaves, broken
100ml (3½fl oz) cold water

Rinse the joint under cold running water and pat dry with kitchen paper. Place the apples in the slow cooker dish. Add the lemon zest and juice and stir well to coat the apple pieces. Add the sugar, thyme, bay leaves and water and mix well.

Place the meat, fat side up, on the apple mixture (it's important that the meat covers the apples completely to prevent them from turning brown). Cover with the lid and cook on low for 8-10 hours.

If you like crackling, preheat your grill to its highest setting. Place the cooked pork under the grill for about 5 minutes or until golden and bubbling. Leave to stand for 5 minutes before carving into thick slices and serve with the apple sauce.

COOKING CONVENTIONALLY?
Preheat the oven to 150°C (330°F), Gas mark 2. Place the pork in a roasting tin just large enough to accommodate it in a single layer and bake in the oven for 5 hours. Increase the temperature to 220°C (425°F), Gas mark 7, for the final 15-20 minutes for the crackling.

Italian milk-fed pork

PREPARATION TIME: 15 MINUTES
COOKING TIME: 6¼-8¼ HOURS
SERVES 4

Cooking pork in milk has been done for years in Italy. It gives the meat a wonderful mild flavour and amazing succulence.

2kg (4lb 7oz) pork loin roast,
  on the bone
2 tbsp olive oil
50g (2oz) butter
1 onion, peeled and sliced
2 celery sticks, trimmed and
  diced

1-1.5 litres (1¾-2½ pints) whole
  milk
4 bay leaves
4 sage leaves
Pared zest of 1 orange
1 cinnamon stick
2 garlic cloves, peeled

Wash the pork under cold running water and pat dry with kitchen paper. Warm a large frying pan over a high heat. When hot add the olive oil and butter, and when melted and bubbling add the meat and cook for 5–10 minutes or until browned all over.

Place the onion and celery in the slow cooker dish and spread out to cover the base. Top with the meat. Deglaze the pan with a little of the milk, stirring to scrape up any crusty bits from the bottom of the pan.

Pour the contents of the pan into the slow cooker. Pour in enough milk to cover the meat, then add the herbs, orange zest, cinnamon and garlic. Cover with the lid and cook for 6–8 hours, turning once, until the pork is cooked and the sauce is curdled (don't worry – it really is supposed to be like that!).

Remove and discard the orange rind, herbs and spices. Remove the pork from the slow cooker and place on a board. Cut the pork into thin slices and arrange on serving plates, then spoon over the curd sauce. Serve with steamed seasonal green vegetables.

I ALSO LIKE...
to cook pork chops on the bone in the same way. Cook for a maximum of 4 hours, using only enough milk to cover the meat.

Rolled roast pork with spiced pear chutney

PREPARATION TIME: 25 MINUTES
COOKING TIME: 6-8 HOURS
SERVES 8

Pork and pears are a classic combination. Here, I have used tinned pears as fresh ones can turn brown during slow cooking - it also makes it a great store-cupboard recipe.

2kg (4lb 7oz) boned and rolled pork shoulder

1 x 400g (14oz) tin pear quarters in natural juice

200ml (7fl oz) dry cider or apple juice

3 tbsp golden caster sugar

1 cinnamon stick

¼ tsp crushed dried chillies

A pinch of freshly grated nutmeg

Sea salt and freshly ground black pepper

FOR THE SPICE PASTE:

2 tsp fennel seeds

1 tsp coriander seeds

¼ tsp black peppercorns

1 tsp dried chilli flakes, or to taste

3 tsp sea salt

4 garlic cloves, peeled and crushed

Finely grated zest and juice of 1 lemon (preferably unwaxed)

Remove the strings from the pork and unroll it. Lay it out flat on a board, fat side upper-most. Using a very sharp knife, score the skin deeply at 1cm (½in) intervals (or ask your butcher to do this for you). Turn the meat over.

To make the spice paste, place the fennel, coriander, peppercorns, chilli flakes, salt, garlic and lemon zest and juice in a food processor or use a mortar and blitz or pound to make a thick paste.

Continued overleaf

Smother the upper side of the meat with two-thirds of the paste and place 3–4 pieces of pear along the left-hand end of the meat. Re-roll the pork from the left-hand side like a Swiss roll, so that the pear quarters are in the centre. Re-tie the meat with fresh kitchen string at 2cm (¾in) intervals and smooth the remaining paste over the outside of the meat.

Dice the remaining pears and add them to the slow cooker dish together with their juice, the cider or apple juice, the sugar, cinnamon, chillies and nutmeg. Mix well, then place the meat on top. Cover with the lid and cook on low for 6–8 hours or until the meat is tender.

If you like crackling, preheat your grill to its highest setting. Place the pork under the grill for about 5 minutes or until golden and bubbling. Leave to stand for 5 minutes before carving into thick slices. Season the pear chutney to taste with salt and pepper and serve with the pork.

I ALSO LIKE...
making sure I've cooked too much so there's plenty left over for pork sandwiches the next day!

Hoisin pork roast

PREPARATION TIME: 5 MINUTES
COOKING TIME: 6–8 HOURS
SERVES 6

This simple recipe tastes great and is perfect for all the family.
Serve with Chinese pancakes, rice or noodles.

1.5 kg (3lb 5oz) boneless pork
    shoulder joint
175g (6oz) hoisin sauce
2 garlic cloves, peeled and
    crushed
1 tbsp grated fresh root ginger
¼ tsp dried chilli flakes

1 tbsp dark soy sauce
2 tsp roasted sesame oil
2 tsp cornflour
2 spring onions, trimmed and
    finely shredded
4 tbsp roughly chopped fresh
    coriander

Wash the meat under cold running water and pat dry with kitchen paper. Mix the hoisin
sauce, garlic, ginger, chilli flakes, soy sauce, sesame oil and cornflour together in the
slow cooker dish. Add the pork and roll it in the mixture until coated. Cover with the lid
and cook on low for 6–8 hours.

Remove the meat from the slow cooker, place on a platter or board and leave to rest
under a tent of foil for 10 minutes.

Skim off any excess fat from the surface of the cooking liquid. Slice the pork and
arrange on a serving platter. Sprinkle the spring onions and coriander over the top and
serve the hot sauce on the side.

I ALSO LIKE...
to use pork belly for this recipe.

Beef in miso

PREPARATION TIME: 10 MINUTES
COOKING TIME: 6½ HOURS
SERVES 6

This Japanese-inspired dish is really easy to make and is wonderfully tasty. After cooking you're left with gorgeously tender meat and a rich, dark miso broth.

2kg (4lb 7oz) beef silverside or topside
10 whole dried shiitake mushrooms
2 tbsp miso paste, plus extra to taste
2 celery sticks, trimmed and diced

100g (3½oz) frozen soya beans, defrosted
Cooked rice noodles, about 50-60g (2-2½oz) per person
Fresh coriander leaves, for sprinkling

Wash the beef under cold running water and pat dry with kitchen paper. Place the shiitake mushrooms in a bowl and pour over enough boiling water to cover. Leave for 5 minutes or until soft. Remove the mushrooms from the water, reserving the flavoured water for later, and slice the mushrooms thickly.

Stir the miso paste into the mushroom-soaking liquid and add this mixture to the slow cooker dish together with the mushrooms and celery. Top with the meat and pour over enough water to come halfway up the meat. Cover with the lid and cook on low for 6 hours or until tender.

Stir in the soya beans and continue cooking, uncovered, for 15–20 minutes or until the beans are tender.

Remove the beef from the slow cooker and cut into wafer-thin slices. Season the 'broth' with more miso to taste. Divide the cooked noodles between six shallow bowls and top with some slices of meat. Ladle over the broth and sprinkle the coriander leaves over to serve.

COOKING CONVENTIONALLY?
Cook in an ovenproof casserole dish with a tight-fitting lid in an oven preheated to 150°C (300°F), Gas mark 2, for 3 hours or until tender.

Italian pot-roast beef

PREPARATION TIME: 15 MINUTES
COOKING TIME: 6¼–8¼ HOURS
SERVES 8

This classic combination of flavours works so well with slow-cooked beef dishes.

1–2kg (2lb 4oz–4lb 7oz) beef chuck roast or pot-roast joint
4 garlic cloves, peeled and halved lengthways
8 fresh rosemary sprigs
Sea salt and freshly ground black pepper
1 tbsp olive oil

1 x 400g (14oz) tin chopped tomatoes
2 tbsp concentrated tomato purée
1 large red onion, peeled and cut into 8 wedges
200ml (7fl oz) red wine

Using a small sharp knife, cut 8 deep slits in the beef. Stuff the slits with the garlic and rosemary and season the meat generously with salt and pepper.

Warm the olive oil in a large frying pan over a high heat. When hot, add the meat and cook for 5–10 minutes or until browned on all sides.

Place the tomatoes, tomato purée and onion in the slow cooker dish and mix well. Top with the seared beef.

Return the pan to the heat and add the red wine, stirring continuously to scrape up any bits from the bottom of the pan. Pour the contents of the pan over the meat. Cover with the lid and cook on low for 6–8 hours or until tender.

Remove the beef from the slow cooker, place on a board and leave to rest for 5–10 minutes.

Skim off any excess fat from the surface of the cooking liquid. Cut the beef into wafer-thin slices and serve with the sauce and vegetables spooned over.

COOKING CONVENTIONALLY?
Preheat the oven to 180°C (350°F), Gas mark 4. Brown the beef in a large ovenproof casserole dish on the hob, then add the remaining ingredients, cover with a tight-fitting lid and cook in the oven for 3 hours or until tender.

Brisket cooked in coffee

PREPARATION TIME: 10 MINUTES
COOKING TIME: 6¼–8¼ HOURS
SERVES 6

This recipe might sound a bit weird, but have faith! I discovered several American recipes that involved slow cooking beef in coffee and thought I really must give it a go – the resulting sauce is rich and tasty, with a wonderful flavour. Definitely worth a try!

1.3kg (2lb 13oz) rolled brisket
  joint
2 carrots, peeled and diced
2 celery sticks, peeled and diced
1 large onion, peeled and diced
2 fresh thyme sprigs

2 tbsp concentrated tomato
  purée
Sea salt and freshly ground black
  pepper
250ml (9fl oz) strong black coffee

Rinse the meat under cold running water and pat dry with kitchen paper. Place the vegetables in the slow cooker dish together with the thyme, then mix in the tomato purée. Top with the meat and season with salt and pepper. Pour the coffee over the top. Cover with the lid and cook on low for 6–8 hours.

Remove the meat from the slow cooker, place on a board and leave to rest under a tent of foil for 5–10 minutes.

Pour the sauce into a saucepan and bring to the boil over a high heat. Boil for about 5–10 minutes or until reduced and starting to thicken. Cut the meat into wafer-thin slices and drizzle with the sauce.

FAB FOR THE FREEZER
Leave to cool completely and then freeze for up to three months. Defrost thoroughly, then carve the meat and gently reheat the sauce on the hob (never in the slow cooker).

Manzo arrosto (stuffed rolled beef)

PREPARATION TIME: 20 MINUTES
COOKING TIME: 5–6 HOURS
SERVES 6

There are all sorts of versions and regional Italian variations of this recipe. This is my hybrid.

1.3kg (2lb 13oz) rolled brisket
  joint
75g (3oz) baby spinach leaves

FOR THE FILLING:
50g (2oz) lean minced beef
25g (1oz) minced pork (or use all
  beef if you'd rather)
1 garlic clove, peeled and crushed
1 tbsp roughly chopped fresh
  parsley leaves
4 tsp finely grated fresh
  Parmesan cheese
2 tbsp fresh breadcrumbs
1 medium egg, beaten
1/4 tsp sea salt
1/2 tbsp olive oil

FOR THE SAUCE:
4 tbsp good-quality olive oil
3 garlic cloves, peeled and
  roughly chopped
4 fresh bay leaves
200ml (7fl oz) white wine
2 tsp sea salt
2 x 400g (14oz) tins whole plum
  tomatoes
4 tbsp concentrated tomato
  purée
6 tbsp roughly chopped fresh
  flat-leaf parsley leaves and
  some tender stalks

Unravel the meat and lay it out flat on a board. Spread the spinach leaves out over the meat as evenly as possible. Place all the filling ingredients together in a bowl and mix well to combine. Press this mixture onto the spinach in an even layer.

Continued overleaf

Roll the meat up tightly to re-form its original shape. Push any stray filling back into the roast as you go, then tie the meat at 2cm (¾in) intervals with kitchen string.

Place all the sauce ingredients in the slow cooker dish and add the meat. Cover with the lid and cook on low for 5–6 hours or until tender.

Remove the meat from the slow cooker, place on a board and leave to rest under a tent of foil for 10 minutes. Leave the sauce cooking on the slow cooker base during this time, uncovered.

Carve the beef into thick slices and serve with the sauce spooned over and with sautéed potatoes.

I ALSO LIKE...
to use any leftover sauce to make a great soup. Blend until smooth and add vegetable stock to reach your preferred consistency.

6

Super slow

Long and luscious tomato sauce

PREPARATION TIME: 15 MINUTES
COOKING TIME: 15-20 HOURS
SERVES 6 (AS A PASTA SAUCE)   VEGETARIAN

The longer you cook this sauce the better!

2 garlic cloves, peeled

Olive oil

2 x 400g (14oz) tins whole plum
  tomatoes

3 tbsp concentrated tomato
  purée

1 very ripe red peppers, deseeded
  and cut into chunks

4 tbsp finely chopped dark green
  celery leaves (optional)

1 tsp fresh thyme leaves

1 large pinch of dried basil

1 dried chilli, stalk snapped off

Sea salt and freshly ground black
  pepper

TO SERVE

Freshly cooked pasta

Finely grated pecorino cheese

Fresh basil leaves

Using your thumb, press each garlic clove firmly to bruise. Add enough olive oil, about 2mm (1⁄16in) in depth, to cover the base of the slow cooker dish.

Place the tomatoes in a large bowl and crush lightly with a potato masher, leaving some texture. Add the tomatoes, tomato purée, red peppers, celery leaves (if using), thyme, basil, chilli and ½ teaspoon of salt to the slow cooker dish. Cover with the lid and cook on low for at least 15 hours or for up to 20 hours or until thick. Add up to 200ml of boiling water to reach your preferred consistency.

Season to taste with 4 tablespoons of olive oil and salt and pepper.

To serve, toss with freshly cooked pasta, with a touch of extra sauce spooned over the top, then sprinkle with finely grated pecorino and whole basil leaves.

I ALSO LIKE...
to add sliced beef leg or shin to this sauce while it cooks – the meat becomes utterly tender and very yummy!

Italian baked beans

PREPARATION TIME: 5 MINUTES, PLUS SOAKING
COOKING TIME: 12 HOURS
SERVES 6

This recipe is based on a traditional Italian peasant dish, but don't be tempted to think therefore that it doesn't taste great – the simple ingredients work amazingly in this recipe, and I absolutely love it!

500g (1lb 2oz) dried haricot beans

A large handful of fresh curly parsley, finely chopped, plus extra to serve

6 garlic cloves, peeled and finely chopped

½ tsp ground cinnamon

¼ tsp ground cloves

¼ tsp ground mace

Sea salt and freshly ground black pepper

1kg (2lb 4oz) pork belly, cut into 6 even-sized pieces

1 x 400g (14oz) tin chopped tomatoes

Place the beans in a large bowl, cover with cold water and leave to soak for 12 hours. The next day, refresh under cold running water and drain well.

Mix the parsley, garlic, cinnamon, cloves, mace and a generous amount of pepper together in the slow cooker dish. Add the pork and turn it over in the mixture until evenly coated. Arrange the pork in a single layer over the base of the slow cooker (it should cover the base).

Scatter the soaked beans over the top of the pork, followed by the tomatoes, but don't stir the mixture. Pour over enough cold water to cover the beans and tomatoes by about 3cm (1¼in). Cover with the lid and cook on low for 12 hours or until the beans are tender.

Season to taste for the first time with salt (doing this earlier will toughen the beans). Ladle into warm bowls and scatter with more chopped parsley. Great served with fresh crusty bread.

Brined and spiced slow-cooked chicken

PREPARATION TIME: 10 MINUTES, PLUS SOAKING
COOKING TIME: 6 HOURS
SERVES 6

The brining of Christmas turkeys to retain moisture seems to be increasingly popular here in the UK, and has been in the States for quite a while. If it works for turkey then why not chicken?

2kg (4lb 7oz) large free-range chicken (or to fit comfortably in your slow cooker dish)

1 orange, halved

1 onion, peeled and quartered

1 bunch of fresh thyme

FOR THE BRINE:
75g (3oz) table salt

200g (7oz) caster sugar

4 bay leaves, broken

1 bunch of fresh thyme

1 head garlic, unpeeled and halved horizontally

1 tbsp allspice berries, lightly crushed

1 tbsp black peppercorns

1 orange, halved

Wash the chicken inside and out with cold running water and pat dry with kitchen paper.

Place all the brine ingredients into the slow cooker dish and add enough cold water to half fill. Stir the mixture until the salt and sugar dissolve, then add the chicken and hold it down so that the cavity fills with water. Top up with more cold water to cover the bird completely. Cover with the lid and place in the fridge for 24 hours.

Remove the chicken from the brine mixture and rinse under cold running water, then pat dry with kitchen paper. Discard the brine and wash the slow cooker dish.

Fill the cavity of the chicken with the orange, onion and thyme and place the chicken in the clean slow cooker dish. Cover with the lid and cook on low for 6 hours or until the juices run clear when tested with a skewer between the leg and the breast.

The bird will be very pale looking, but remove the skin to reveal the gorgeous succulent meat within. Serve with the cooking juices spooned over.

24-hour Hungarian pork

PREPARATION TIME: 10 MINUTES
COOKING TIME: 24 HOURS
SERVES 8

Try this wonderfully tasty and moist pork dish – perfect for a main course, or also great hot or cold in sandwiches.

3 kg (2lb 13oz) bone-in shoulder of pork (or a size to fit in your slow cooker dish)

5 garlic cloves, peeled

2 tsp smoked paprika

A large pinch of dried chilli flakes, or to taste

1 tsp caraway seeds

1 tbsp dark brown muscovado sugar

½ tsp sea salt

2 tbsp concentrated tomato purée

4 tbsp cold water

5 tbsp soured cream

Sea salt and freshly ground black pepper

Rinse the pork under cold running water and pat dry with kitchen paper. Place in the slow cooker dish.

Place the garlic, paprika, chilli flakes, caraway seeds, sugar, salt, tomato purée and water into a food processor and blitz to make a thick paste. Alternatively, use a pestle and mortar. Rub the paste all over the pork. Cover with the lid and cook on low for 24 hours or until gloriously tender.

Remove the pork from the slow cooker and place on a plate or board. Use 2 forks to remove any large pieces of fat and discard. Use the forks to divide the meat into large pieces.

Skim off any excess fat from the surface of the cooking liquid. Stir in the soured cream and season to taste with salt and pepper. Drizzle the cooking juices over the meat before serving with new potatoes and salad.

FAB FOR THE FREEZER
Leave the meat to cool in the sauce without adding the soured cream. The fat will harden, making it easier to remove. Freeze the meat for up to three months. Defrost thoroughly, before reheating in the sauce gently on the hob until piping hot. Add the soured cream and stir through.

Lamb with 40 cloves of garlic

PREPARATION TIME: 5 MINUTES
COOKING TIME: 16 HOURS
SERVES 4-6

I've seen many recipes over the years for chicken with 40 cloves, but thought I would give lamb a try instead. I'm pleased to report that it's amazing and perfect for the slow cooker!

1.5-2kg (3lb 5oz-4lb 7oz) shoulder of lamb, bone in (depending on the size of your slow cooker dish - you want the lamb to completely cover the base)
1 tsp paprika
1 tsp fennel seeds (optional)

1 large onion, peeled and finely sliced
40 garlic cloves (about 3-5 whole heads), peeled
Sea salt and freshly ground black pepper

Wash the lamb under cold running water and pat dry with kitchen paper. Rub the meat with the paprika and fennel.

Place the onion in the slow cooker dish, spreading it evenly over the base. Press each garlic clove with your thumb or the back of a knife to just break the surface of each one, but not crush them, and scatter over the onion.

Position the meat over the garlic, fat side up. Cover with the lid and cook on low for 16 hours or until falling off the bone.

Remove the meat from the slow cooker and place on a plate or board. Use 2 forks to shred the meat.

Skim off any excess fat from the surface of the cooking juices. Season to taste with salt and pepper, then serve the meat with the gorgeous cooking juices spooned over.

I ALSO LIKE...
making this recipe with a large bone-in pork roast.

24-hour lamb salad with pine nuts and sultanas

PREPARATION TIME: 20 MINUTES, PLUS STANDING
COOKING TIME: 24 HOURS
SERVES 6

Cooking lamb long and slow works brilliantly, but the secret for super slow cooking is to make sure the meat is on the bone – this will give you guaranteed succulence and stop the meat from drying out. Here the lamb is served in a salad, but you could serve it on its own, topped with the pine nuts if you prefer.

1.5kg (3lb 5oz) lamb shoulder bone in (the meat must cover the slow cooker base completely)

2 large pinches of saffron strands

2 tbsp warm water

2 garlic cloves, peeled and roughly chopped

1 tsp ground ginger

1 red chilli, trimmed and roughly chopped

1 tsp cumin seeds

75g (3oz) sultanas

300g (10oz) mixed baby salad leaves

50g (2oz) pine nuts, toasted

Sea salt and freshly ground black pepper

Place the lamb in the slow cooker dish fat side up (the meat should cover the whole of the base of the slow cooker dish). Place the saffron and warm water in a small bowl and leave to soak.

Meanwhile, place all the remaining ingredients, except the sultanas, salad leaves and pine nuts, in a food processor and blitz to make a rough paste. Add the saffron and its soaking water and blitz again to combine.

Rub the paste over the upper surface of the lamb. Cover with the lid and cook on low for 24 hours.

Carefully remove the meat from the slow cooker, place on a plate and leave to rest while you prepare the remaining ingredients. Skim off and discard any excess fat from the surface of the cooking liquid. Pour the remaining juices into a wide bowl and add

Continued overleaf

the sultanas. Leave to stand for 10 minutes. Meanwhile, place the salad leaves on a large platter. Use 2 forks to shred the meltingly tender lamb, and remove any bones. Place the meat in the cooling sauce and season to taste with salt and pepper. Scatter the meat over the salad leaves and top with the pine nuts.

Traditional osso bucco with gremolata

PREPARATION TIME: 15 MINUTES
COOKING TIME: 12¼ HOURS
SERVES 4

In Italian, *osso bucco* means 'bone with a hole'. Traditionally veal shin is used for this dish, cut horizontally through the bone, revealing the marrowbone-filled hole in the centre.

4 osso bucco (veal shin), about 1kg (2lb 4oz)
2 tbsp plain flour, for dusting
Sea salt and freshly ground black pepper
2 tbsp olive oil
25g (1oz) butter
1 small onion, peeled and very finely chopped
1 celery stick, trimmed and finely chopped

150ml (5fl oz) dry white wine
200ml (7fl oz) hot chicken or vegetable stock

FOR THE GREMOLATA:
Finely grated zest of 1 lemon (preferably unwaxed)
½ garlic clove, peeled and finely chopped
1 tbsp finely chopped fresh parsley

Rinse the meat under cold running water and pat dry with kitchen paper. Place the flour and some salt and pepper on a large plate. Add the meat and dust each piece to coat evenly, being careful not to dislodge any of the precious marrow.

Warm the olive oil in a large frying pan over a high heat. When hot, add the meat and cook for about 5 minutes on each side or until browned. Remove from the pan with tongs and set aside.

Reduce the heat to medium and add the butter. Add the onion, celery and a pinch of salt to the pan and cook gently, stirring frequently, for 5 minutes or until the vegetables are softened but not coloured. Tip the vegetables and any pan juices into the slow cooker dish and spread out to cover the base. Top with the meat (in a single layer if you can) and any juices that have gathered while it has been resting, then pour over the wine and stock. Cover with the lid and cook on low for 12 hours or until the meat is tender and falling off the bone.

Just before you are ready to eat, mix all the gremolata ingredients together and sprinkle it over the osso bucco before serving with creamy, Parmesan-rich polenta.

COOKING CONVENTIONALLY?
Preheat the oven to 150°C (300°F), Gas mark 2. After browning, place the meat in an ovenproof casserole dish with a tight-fitting lid and cook in the oven for 3 hours until the meat is coming off the bone, turning the meat every 20 minutes or so. When turning, lift the meat gently with a spatula so that it stays in one piece and the marrow is not lost.

Spicy pulled pork with red onion chutney

PREPARATION TIME: 10 MINUTES, PLUS MARINATING
COOKING TIME: 16 HOURS
SERVES 8

This simple recipe tastes great!

2kg (4lb 7oz) pork shoulder (off-the bone)
1 tbsp dried chilli flakes
1 tsp dried oregano
2 tbsp soft dark brown sugar, plus extra to taste
1 tsp sea salt
1 tsp chipotle chilli (smoked chilli) paste (optional)

100ml (3½fl oz) red wine vinegar
2 red onions, peeled and finely sliced
6 garlic cloves, peeled and sliced
Sea salt and freshly ground black pepper

Place the pork in a dish and rub the meat with the chilli flakes, oregano, half the sugar, salt, chilli paste (if using) and vinegar. Cover and marinate in the fridge for at least 4 hours or for up to 24 hours.

Place the remaining sugar, onions and garlic in the base of the slow cooker dish and mix well. Top with the marinated pork. Cover with the lid and cook on low for 16 hours.

Remove the pork from the slow cooker and place on a platter or board. Use 2 forks to shred the meat, discarding any large pieces of fat. Moisten the meat with the pan juices.

Season the onions in the slow cooker and add sugar to taste. Serve the pork in crusty rolls or wraps with the red onion chutney and some rocket leaves.

FAB FOR THE FREEZER
Place the shredded pork and onion chutney in separate freezerproof containers and freeze for up to three months. Defrost thoroughly before using at room temperature, or reheat gently on the hob until piping hot.

Bourbon-soaked beef

PREPARATION TIME: 10 MINUTES
COOKING TIME: 12–16 HOURS
SERVES 8–10

This recipe is simple to make, but tastes amazing.

**2.5kg (5lb 8oz) beef shin or leg
  meat, sliced
2 onions, peeled and finely sliced
1 red pepper, deseeded and finely
  sliced
1 beef stock cube
2 tbsp concentrated tomato
  purée
250ml (9fl oz) bourbon
Sea salt and freshly ground black
  pepper
Roughly chopped fresh flat-leaf
  parsley, for sprinkling**

Rinse the beef under cold running water and pat dry with kitchen paper.

Scatter the onions and red pepper over the base of the slow cooker dish. Crumble over
the stock cube and stir in the tomato purée and bourbon. Top with the beef in a single
layer if possible, nestling it in tightly, and season with salt and pepper. Cover with the
lid and cook on low for 12–16 hours.

Mix the meat with the sauce; the beef will break up a little, but this is what you want!
Sprinkle over the parsley and season to taste. Serve with crusty bread or rice.

I ALSO LIKE...
to make this recipe using a rolled brisket joint.

Salt beef

PREPARATION TIME: 20 MINUTES, PLUS 6–11 DAYS MARINATING
COOKING TIME: 6 HOURS 10 MINUTES
SERVES 4

This recipe is in the super slow chapter for a reason ... you will need to start this recipe about 11 days before you wish to eat it, but it is worth the wait!

2–3kg (4lb 7oz–2lb 13oz) beef
  brisket, unrolled
300g (10oz) rock salt
150g (5oz) soft muscovado sugar
1 tbsp black peppercorns
1 tbsp coriander seeds
1 tbsp juniper berries

2 bay leaves
¼ tsp ground mace
½ tsp ground ginger
2 carrots, peeled and cut into
  chunks
2 celery sticks, trimmed and cut
  into chunks

Place the beef and half of the salt in a large freezer bag or sealed container and leave in the fridge for 12 hours. Rinse the meat under cold running water and pat dry with kitchen paper.

Place the remaining salt in a food processor with the sugar, peppercorns, coriander, juniper, bay leaves, mace and ginger and blitz to make a powder. Rub this mixture into the beef until thoroughly coated.

Place the beef in a clean freezer bag or sealed container and leave in the fridge for 5–10 days (the longer the better), turning the meat once or twice a day. Rinse the salt off the meat with cold running water.

Bring a large saucepan of water to the boil. Gently slide the meat into the water and simmer for 5 minutes. Place the carrots and celery in the slow cooker dish. Using a slotted spoon and some tongs, remove the meat from the water and place in the slow cooker on the bed of vegetables. Cover with the lid and cook on low for 6 hours or until very tender.

Remove the beef from the slow cooker and eat warm or leave to cool. Cut into thin slices to serve.

Roman oxtail

PREPARATION TIME: 15 MINUTES
COOKING TIME: 16½–20½ HOURS
SERVES 6

Not knowing otherwise, I have for years been adding red wine to Italian tomato-based sauces. With a few trips to Italy and some research into Italian food I discovered that dry white wine is often used instead. Here is my version of a classic dish served in Rome.

1kg (2lb 4oz) beef oxtail
4 tbsp olive oil
4 celery sticks, trimmed and finely chopped
1 garlic clove, peeled and finely chopped
1 large carrot, peeled and finely chopped
1 medium white onion, peeled and finely chopped
75g (3oz) pancetta, finely chopped

3 tbsp finely chopped fresh flat-leaf parsley
250ml dry white wine
1 tbsp concentrated tomato purée
2 x 400g (14oz) tins chopped tomatoes
5 whole cloves
1 bay leaf, broken
Sea salt and freshly ground black pepper

Rinse the oxtail under cold running water and pat dry with kitchen paper.

Warm the olive oil in a large frying pan over a medium heat. When hot, add the vegetables, pancetta and 1 tablespoon of the parsley. Mix well and fry for 4–5 minutes or until softened. Spoon the vegetables into the slow cooker dish.

Return the pan to the heat and add the oxtail. Cook for 10–15 minutes, turning the pieces regularly, until well browned.

Add the wine and bring to the boil for 1–2 minutes, stirring to scrape any bits from the bottom of the pan. Pour into the slow cooker.

Continued overleaf

Add the tomato purée, tomatoes, cloves and bay leaf and mix well. Add just enough cold water to cover the oxtail. Cover with the lid and cook for at least 16 hours or for up to 20 hours.

Stir in the remaining parsley and season to taste with salt and pepper. Spoon into deep plates or soup bowls to serve.

COOKING CONVENTIONALLY?
Cook the vegetables and browned oxtail in a large ovenproof casserole dish with a tight-fitting lid for 6–8 hours in an oven preheated to 140°C (275°F), Gas mark 1, until rich and tender.

Ox cheeks in ale with barley and herb dumplings

PREPARATION TIME: 15 MINUTES
COOKING TIME: 12 HOURS 10 MINUTES
SERVES 4-6

This rich and tasty stew is very economical to make. Check that your slow cooker dish can go in the oven before making the dumplings.

2 ox cheeks (about 950g/2lb in
  total), diced into 3cm (1¼in)
  chunks
2 tbsp plain flour
Sea salt and freshly ground black
  pepper
4 tbsp olive oil
500ml (18fl oz) ale
2 celery sticks, trimmed and cut
  into 2-3cm (¾-1¼in) chunks
1 large carrot, peeled and cut into
  2-3cm (¾-1¼in) chunks
1 leek, trimmed and cut into 2cm
  (¾in) chunks
25g (1oz) pearl barley
3 tbsp Worcestershire sauce
4 whole garlic cloves, peeled
2 fresh rosemary sprigs

FOR THE DUMPLINGS:
150g (5oz) self-raising flour, plus
  extra for dusting
75g (3oz) suet
2 tbsp roughly chopped fresh
  mixed herbs, such as parsley,
  mint and basil
About 100ml (3½fl oz) cold water

Pat the meat dry with kitchen paper. Place in a freezer bag with the flour and some salt and pepper. Seal the top and shake to coat the meat evenly.

Warm the olive oil in a large frying pan, and when hot add the meat and cook for 3-5 minutes until browned. Add 2 tablespoons of the ale to deglaze the pan, stirring to scrape up all the caramelised bits from the bottom. Tip into the slow cooker dish.

Continued overleaf

Add the celery, carrot, leek and barley to the slow cooker dish together with the Worcestershire sauce, garlic and rosemary and mix well. Cover with the lid and cook on low for 12 hours.

Stir well, then remove and discard the rosemary and season to taste with salt and pepper.

About an hour before you wish to eat, prepare the dumplings. Preheat your oven to 190°C (375°F), Gas mark 5. Using your hands, mix the flour, suet and herbs together in a large bowl. Season and add just enough water to bring the mixture together into a firm dough.

Roll the dough into 6–8 balls, dusting your hands with flour if the dough becomes sticky. Drop the dough balls onto the top of the beef mixture and place uncovered in the hot oven. Cook for 20–30 minutes or until golden and well risen.

COOKING CONVENTIONALLY?
Preheat the oven to 120°C (250°F), Gas mark ½. Brown the beef, place in a large ovenproof casserole dish with a tight-fitting lid and cook in the oven for 12 hours until piping hot and thick. Increase the temperature to 190°C (375°F), Gas mark 5, to cook the dumplings.

7

Feasts

Celebration Easter lamb

PREPARATION TIME: 15 MINUTES
COOKING TIME: 6¼ HOURS
SERVES 8-10

This all-in-one dish is ideal for a celebration or party as all the preparation is done in advance and kept contained in one pot.

2kg (4lb 7oz) leg of lamb on the bone (or to fit in your slow cooker dish)
2 tbsp olive oil
500g (1lb 2oz) baby new potatoes, scrubbed
750g (1lb 10oz) baby carrots, scrubbed
2 red onions, peeled and cut into wedges

3 fresh mint sprigs
2 fresh rosemary sprigs
4 tbsp red wine vinegar
6 garlic cloves, peeled and roughly chopped
250ml (9fl oz) lamb stock
Sea salt and freshly ground black pepper

Rinse the lamb under cold running water and pat dry with kitchen paper.

Warm the olive oil in a large frying pan over a high heat. When hot, add the lamb and cook for 10 minutes or until browned all over. Place the lamb in the slow cooker dish. Scatter the new potatoes around the meat, then top with the carrots and onions to surround the meat. Sprinkle over the herbs, vinegar and garlic, then pour over the stock. Cover with the lid and cook on low for 6 hours or until the meat is tender.

Remove the meat from the slow cooker, place on a board and leave to rest under a tent of foil for 5–15 minutes.

Season the vegetables to taste with salt and pepper and remove and discard the herbs. Carve the lamb and serve with the vegetables and the cooking juices spooned over.

I ALSO LIKE...
to roast a rolled shoulder of lamb in this way if I need to leave the meat for longer. The shoulder has more fat so won't dry out like the leg will over 8–9 hours of cooking.

Party paella for a crowd

PREPARATION TIME: 20 MINUTES
COOKING TIME: 4½–5½ HOURS
SERVES 10

I love paella, but it can overcook without lots of careful watching. The slow cooker takes all the hassle out of it, giving you plenty of time to prepare and resulting in an easy, hot meal for a crowd a few hours later. Perfect! You will need a large 5–6 litre (9–10½ pint) slow cooker for this quantity, or adjust the amounts accordingly.

2 tbsp olive oil

200g (7oz) chorizo, cut into chunks

4 garlic cloves, peeled and finely chopped

2 onions, peeled and finely diced

2 red peppers, deseeded and diced

1½ tsp fresh thyme leaves

½ tsp dried chilli flakes

1 tsp paprika

750ml (1¼ pints) long grain rice

200ml (7fl oz) dry white wine

1 litre (1¾ pints) chicken stock

A large pinch of saffron strands

150g (5oz) frozen petit pois

1 x 400g (14oz) tin chopped tomatoes, drained (keep the juice for cooking or for a Bloody Mary the morning after the party!)

10 chicken thighs, skinned

25g (1oz) butter

20 large raw shell-on prawns

30 small clams, cleaned (optional)

6 tbsp finely chopped fresh flat-leaf parsley

Sea salt and freshly ground black pepper

Warm half the olive oil in a large frying pan over a high heat. When hot, add the chorizo and cook for 5 minutes or until the orangey oils are released. Add three-quarters of the garlic, the onions and red peppers and continue cooking for a further 5 minutes or until soft. Mix in the thyme, chilli flakes and paprika, then spoon into the slow cooker dish with any cooking juices. Add the rice, wine, stock, saffron, peas, tomatoes and

Continued overleaf

chicken and mix well. Cover with the lid and cook on low for 4–5 hours or until the liquid has been absorbed and the rice is tender.

Warm the remaining olive oil and the butter together in a large clean frying pan over a high heat. When hot, add the reserved garlic, followed by the prawns and clams (if using) and cook for 5–10 minutes, shaking the pan occasionally, until all the prawns are pink and the clams have opened. Discard any unopened clams.

Stir the parsley into the rice and season to taste. Distribute the hot shellfish over the top together with any pan juices, and serve immediately.

I ALSO LIKE...
to add rabbit pieces on the bone to this dish – add them instead of, or as well as, the chicken.

Black velvet celebration 'pies'

PREPARATION TIME: 25 MINUTES
COOKING TIME: 10½–15½ HOURS
SERVES 8

These individual pies are a bit of a cheat really as you cook the pastry separately, but they taste great and are perfect when feeding a crowd.

1.5kg (3lb 5oz) diced braising steak

3 tbsp plain flour, plus extra for dusting

1 tsp English mustard powder

3 tbsp olive oil

18 baby shallots, peeled

1 large carrot, peeled and finely diced

1 large celery stick, trimmed and finely diced

300g (10oz) baby button mushrooms, cleaned and trimmed

2 tbsp concentrated tomato purée

300ml (10fl oz) Guinness

250ml (9fl oz) brut dry champagne or dry sparkling wine

500g (1lb 2oz) puff pastry

2 tbsp milk, for glazing

75g (3oz) Irish blue cheese, cut into cubes

Sea salt and freshly ground black pepper

Pat the diced beef dry with kitchen paper and place in a large freezer bag together with the flour and mustard powder. Seal the top and shake well to coat the meat.

Warm a third of the olive oil in a large frying pan over a high heat. When hot, add the beef, in batches if necessary, and cook until well browned all over. Place in the slow cooker dish.

Continued overleaf

Return the pan to the heat and add another third of the oil and the shallots. Cook for about 5 minutes or until evenly browned. Add to the slow cooker, then repeat the process with the rest of the oil and the mushrooms, cooking for 5 minutes or until no more liquid remains in the pan.

Mix the vegetables (including the cooked mushrooms), tomato purée, Guinness and champagne or wine into the meat mixture. Cover with the lid and cook on low for 10–15 hours or until rich and tender.

About half an hour before the beef is ready or you wish to eat, preheat the oven to 190°C (375°F), Gas mark 5. Roll out the pastry on a well-floured surface until it is about 5mm (¼in) thick. Using a round cutter, stamp out 6 circles each about 10cm (4in) across. Using the tip of a sharp knife, score the tops with a criss-cross pattern.

Place the pastry circles on a non-stick baking tray. Brush with a little milk to glaze and cook in the oven for 10–15 minutes or until golden and risen.

Five minutes before serving, mix the blue cheese into the meat mixture and leave it to melt into the sauce. Season to taste with salt and pepper. Spoon the meat onto serving plates and top each one with a hot pastry circle. Serve with buttered green veggies and some colcannon.

I ALSO LIKE...
to roll, cut and cook the pastry circles in advance, and store in an airtight container for up to three days. Reheat for about 3–5 minutes in an oven preheated to 190°C (375°F), Gas mark 5, when ready to eat.

Bonfire night sausage hotpot

PREPARATION TIME: 15 MINUTES

COOKING TIME: 6¼–8¼ HOURS

SERVES 8

This easy recipe is a real crowd pleaser, especially on a cold bonfire night.

1 tbsp olive oil

1 large onion, peeled and chopped

16 good-quality pork and herb sausages

2 red peppers, deseeded and cut into cubes

1 x 400g (14oz) tin chopped tomatoes

2 x 400g (14oz) tins mixed beans in water, rinsed and drained

2 red chillies, deseeded and finely chopped (leave the seeds in if you like it spicy!)

3 tbsp tomato purée

1 vegetable stock cube

1 tsp Worcestershire sauce

1 tsp dark muscovado sugar, plus extra to taste

2 fresh thyme sprigs

2 fresh rosemary sprigs

Warm the olive oil in a large frying pan over a medium heat. When hot, add the onion and fry for 5 minutes or until softened. Transfer the onion to the slow cooker dish.

Return the pan to the heat and add the sausages. Cook for 5–10 minutes until browned all over. Place them in the slow cooker together with all the remaining ingredients and mix well. Cover with the lid and cook on low for 6–8 hours or until the sauce is thick and flavoursome.

Serve with mash or baked potatoes.

I ALSO LIKE...

making this recipe with bone-in pork chops – brown them instead of the sausages, then add to the slow cooker. Cook on low for 4–6 hours.

Cranberry and chestnut festive turkey crown

PREPARATION TIME: 15 MINUTES
COOKING TIME: 4¼–6¼ HOURS
SERVES 8–10

Cooking the turkey on Christmas day seems to be a major cause of culinary stress! With a slow cooker, concerns of having a dry roast or overcooking can be allayed, as the meat stays gorgeously moist. As the breast meat takes less time to cook than the legs it makes sense to remove one or other and cook them separately for the best results.

2–3kg (4lb 7oz–2lb 13oz) free-range turkey crown (depending on the size of your slow cooker dish)
50g (2oz) dried cranberries
50g (2oz) cooked and peeled chestnuts
25g (1oz) smoked streaky bacon, finely diced

2 tbsp chopped fresh flat-leaf parsley
Sea salt and freshly ground black pepper
1 onion, peeled and finely sliced
100ml (3½fl oz) dry white wine
2 tbsp crème fraîche

Place the turkey on a board and push your hand between the skin and the breast, either side of the backbone, to make 2 pockets.

Place the cranberries, chestnuts and bacon into a food processor and pulse very briefly to combine the ingredients. Stir in the parsley and season to taste with salt and pepper.

Using your hands, push the cranberry stuffing into the 2 pockets that you made earlier under the turkey skin. Divide it evenly between each side, being sure to push it all the way along each breast.

Spread the onion over the base of the slow cooker dish and top with the turkey. Cover with the lid and cook on low for 4–6 hours or until the juices run clear when the deepest part of the flesh is tested with a skewer.

Lift the crown out of the dish, cover and keep in a warm place to rest for at least 15 minutes or for up to 30 minutes.

Meanwhile, skim off any excess fat from the surface of the cooking juices. Pour the remaining juices into a saucepan and bring to the boil over a high heat. Add the wine and continue to boil for another 5 minutes or until reduced by at least half. Season to taste with salt and pepper, then stir in the crème fraîche.

To serve, carefully remove the skin from the turkey breast to reveal the stuffing underneath. Spoon the stuffing onto serving plates before carving the meat. Drizzle with the creamy sauce and serve with all the usual Christmas trimmings.

I ALSO LIKE...
to use a small quantity of my chestnut and chorizo stuffing (see page 145) to push under the turkey skin instead.

Turkey ballotine with chestnuts and port

PREPARATION TIME: 25 MINUTES, PLUS CHILLING
COOKING TIME: 6¼ HOURS, PLUS PREHEATING
SERVES 2

This recipe works really well in the slow cooker and stays wonderfully moist. It is delicious served with roast parsnips and baby carrots.

25g (1oz) butter, chilled and diced

75g (3oz) cooked and peeled chestnuts, finely chopped

1 shallot, peeled and finely chopped

Sea salt and freshly ground black pepper

2 tbsp port

1 large turkey leg or thigh joint, about 800g (1lb 12oz)

125g (4½oz) good-quality sausage meat

2 tbsp chopped fresh parsley

100ml (3½fl oz) dry white wine

1 bay leaf

2 tbsp double cream

Melt half of the butter in a frying pan over a medium heat. Add the chestnuts and shallot and sauté for about 5 minutes or until softened and just starting to colour. Season well with salt and pepper, then add the port and cook for a minute or until reduced. Leave to cool.

Using a sharp knife, cut the turkey leg lengthways down to the bone, using short delicate strokes to cut the meat away from the bone and being careful not to puncture the skin. Remove the bone and set aside, covered, in the fridge for later. Open the leg meat out like a book and lay it skin side down on a board. Use the same light strokes to remove any tough cartilage or smaller bones.

Place the sausage meat in a bowl together with the cooled chestnut mixture and the parsley. Mix well and season to taste. Spread the mixture onto the turkey meat, then roll the meat up firmly like a Swiss roll. Season the skin with salt and pepper. Wrap the turkey roll very tightly in several layers of foil and twist the ends tightly like a sweet to seal. Place in the fridge for at least 12 hours or for up to 24 hours.

To cook, cover the base of the slow cooker with about 5mm (¼in) cold water and add the wine. Cover with the lid and preheat the slow cooker on high for 30 minutes.

Add the bay leaf to the hot mixture in the slow cooker. Reduce the temperature to low and place the foil parcel and the reserved turkey bone (if it will fit) in the slow cooker dish. Cover with the lid and cook on low for 6 hours, turning the parcel over halfway through, until tender and there is no more pink meat.

Carefully remove the parcel from the slow cooker with tongs, place on a board and leave to stand for 10–15 minutes before unwrapping and cutting into thick slices.

To make a simple gravy, discard the bone, then strain the juices from the parcel and the slow cooker dish through a sieve into a small saucepan. Bring to the boil over a high heat and boil rapidly for 2 minutes. Slowly whisk in the cream. Serve the turkey in slices with the gravy spooned over, and all the usual festive veg and trimmings.

COOKING CONVENTIONALLY?
Preheat the oven to 180°C (350°F), Gas mark 4. Place the foil parcel in a small roasting tin and cook in the oven for 45 minutes. Reduce the temperature to 160°C (325°F), Gas mark 3, and continue cooking for a further 45 minutes.

Steamed mincemeat and orange pudding

PREPARATION TIME: 20 MINUTES
COOKING TIME: 3-4 HOURS
SERVES 6

Not everyone likes Christmas pudding, so this sponge is a perfect alternative – it's pretty good on non-festive days too! For a vegetarian version, use a suitable mincemeat.

175g (6oz) butter, softened, plus
  extra for greasing
6 tbsp good-quality mincemeat
175g (6oz) golden caster sugar
175g (6oz) self-raising flour

1 tsp baking powder
3 large eggs
Finely grated zest of 1 orange
1-2 tbsp milk

Butter a 1.2 litre (2 pint) pudding basin (make sure it will fit into your slow cooker dish first – if not make mini ones in ramekins) with butter. Spoon the mincemeat into the base of the pudding basin.

Place the softened butter, sugar, flour, baking powder, eggs and orange zest in a large mixing bowl and beat together well with a wooden spoon or electric food mixer, adding a little milk to loosen the mixture until it drops easily from the spoon or whisk. Spoon the mixture into the basin, on top of the mincemeat.

Butter a large piece of foil and make a pleat in the centre. Press this over the basin, buttered side down, and press down firmly to seal. Tie around the top with kitchen string, and make a string handle so it's easier to lift the pudding in and out of the slow cooker. Scrunch up some foil to make a small cushion on which to rest the pudding basin. Place this in the slow cooker and top with the pudding. Carefully pour enough boiling water around the outside to come about halfway up the sides of the basin. Cover with the lid and cook on high for 3–4 hours or until a skewer pushed into the centre comes out clean.

Unwrap, then run a knife around the edge of the pudding and invert onto a plate. Serve warm with some cream.

Spiced cranberry and ruby port mincemeat

PREPARATION TIME: 10 MINUTES
COOKING TIME: 4 HOURS
MAKES 500ML (18FL OZ)   VEGETARIAN

Cranberries and port are a classic Christmas combination, so I couldn't resist using them in this cooked, suet-free mincemeat.

325g (11oz) cranberries

4 tbsp ruby port

25ml (1fl oz) kirsch

100g (3½oz) soft dark brown
  sugar

1 cinnamon stick

1 vanilla pod, split in half
  lengthways

1 tsp ground ginger

¼ tsp ground cloves

75g (3oz) raisins

75g (3oz) sultanas

50g (2oz) dried cranberries

Finely grated zest and juice of
  1 orange

Place all the ingredients in the slow cooker dish. Cover with the lid and cook on low for 4 hours, removing the lid for the final hour, until thickened and the cranberries are breaking down.

Beat the mixture well with a wooden spoon (being careful of splashes as the sugary mixture will be scaldingly hot). Using tongs, remove the cinnamon and vanilla. Spoon the mixture into sterilised jars and seal with jam covers and lids. Store in the fridge for up to 14 days.

FAB FOR THE FREEZER
If you don't want jars cluttering up the fridge at Christmas, spoon the cooled mincemeat into a container and freeze for up to three months. Defrost thoroughly before using.

All jams, preserves, chutneys and relishes must be potted in very clean, sterilised containers. Wash jars and bottles thoroughly in hot soapy water and dry in an oven preheated to 150°C (300°F), Gas mark 2 (make sure you don't put any plastic seals or

Continued overleaf

lids in the oven as they will melt). After drying, handle the containers as little as possible and leave on a clean tea towel. When the chutney, mincemeat or similar is cooked, pour the hot mixture into the prepared containers while they are still warm (this will lessen the chance of the glass cracking) and fill them almost to the top.

Brandy sauce

PREPARATION TIME: 2 MINUTES
COOKING TIME: 2 HOURS
SERVES 6   VEGETARIAN

It is easy to make brandy sauce on the hob but it requires constant stirring. This method couldn't be easier and leaves you free to do other things.

2 tbsp brandy
1 tbsp cornflour
250ml (9fl oz) whole milk

100ml (3½fl oz) double cream
2 tbsp caster sugar, or to taste

Place the brandy and cornflour in the slow cooker dish and mix well to make a paste. Slowly stir in the milk, cream and sugar. The mixture must cover the base of the slow cooker by at least 2cm (¾in) to prevent it from burning. Cover with the lid and cook on low for 2 hours or until thickened. Whisk well to combine and serve.

I ALSO LIKE...
to use this method with Grand Marnier, Cointreau or other liqueurs.

Easy Christmas pudding

PREPARATION TIME: 15 MINUTES, PLUS SOAKING
COOKING TIME: 6-10 HOURS
SERVES 6-8   VEGETARIAN

This pudding is SO easy to make and tastes great. The slow cooker makes easy work of the cooking, as you won't need to continually check to see if it has boiled dry – it won't!

100g (3½oz) butter, softened, plus
  extra for greasing
100g (3½oz) ready-to-eat dried
  figs
100g (3½oz) ready-to-eat dried
  prunes
100g (3½oz) ready-to-eat dried
  apricots
100g (3½oz) ready-to-eat dried
  cranberries

100g (3½oz) sultanas
4 tbsp Marsala or brandy
Zest and juice of 2 oranges
75g (3oz) white breadcrumbs
75g (3oz) plain flour
2 tsp ground mixed spice
50g (2oz) roughly chopped
  blanched almonds
200g (7oz) soft light brown sugar
2 large eggs

Generously butter a 1.2 litre (2 pint) pudding basin (check that this will fit into your slow cooker dish first) and line the bottom with a small square piece of buttered foil. Chop the figs, prunes and apricots into small 5mm (¼in) pieces (about the same size as the sultanas) and place in a large mixing bowl together with the remaining fruit. Pour over the Marsala or brandy and orange juice, mix well and cover. Leave overnight or until all the liquid is absorbed.

The next day, add the remaining ingredients to the boozy fruit and beat until smooth. Spoon the mixture into the prepared pudding basin. Lightly butter a piece of foil and make a pleat in the centre to allow the pudding to rise. Press this tightly over the pudding basin and push the foil down around the edges. Tie in place with kitchen string, and make a string handle to make lifting the hot basin in and out of the slow cooker easier.

Continued overleaf

Scrunch up some foil to make a small cushion on which to rest the pudding basin. Place this in the slow cooker dish and top with the pudding. Carefully pour enough boiling water around the outside to come about halfway up the sides of the basin. Cover with the lid and cook on high for 6–10 hours (6 hours will produce a light pudding, and it will become darker and richer as the time passes).

Remove the basin from the slow cooker and place on a heatproof surface. Unwrap the pudding and discard the foil. Run the tip of a knife around the edge to loosen, then, using a tea towel to protect your hands, carefully invert the pudding onto a plate to turn out. Serve warm with brandy sauce (see page 142).

I ALSO LIKE...
to get organised by making this pudding in advance. You can make it up to two months ahead. After cooking, leave the pudding to cool completely, then discard the foil and replace with a new piece. Store in the fridge or freezer until needed (if freezing, defrost thoroughly before reheating). To reheat the pudding on Christmas Day, cook for about 2 hours or until piping hot, then invert over a plate and serve.

Paprika chicken with chorizo *see page* 75

(above) **Traditional osso bucco with gremolata** *see page* 120–21

(right) **Spicy pulled pork with red onion chutney** *see page* 122

(above) **Turkey ballotine with chestnuts and port** *see page 138–39*

(left) **Ox cheeks in ale with barley and herb dumplings** *see page 127–28*

(above) **Black velvet celebration 'pies'** *see page 133–34*

(right) **St Clements cheesecake** *see page 159*

Crunchy vanilla and crème caramels *see page 161–62*

Easy chestnut and chorizo stuffing

PREPARATION TIME: 15 MINUTES
COOKING TIME: 4½–6½ HOURS, PLUS COOLING
SERVES 12

This stuffing will cook quickly in the oven, but if you need to free up oven space on Christmas Day, as I always do, then the slow cooker is the answer. I use vacuum-packed cooked and peeled chestnuts for this recipe.

100g (3½oz) butter

1 large onion, peeled and finely diced

100g (3½oz) chorizo, finely diced

A large handful of fresh flat-leaf parsley, finely diced

250g (9oz) cooked and peeled chestnuts

300g (10oz) fresh breadcrumbs

1 x 400g (14oz) tin unsweetened chestnut purée

1/4 tsp freshly grated nutmeg

2 eggs, beaten

Sea salt and freshly ground black pepper

Butter the inside of the slow cooker dish generously with a quarter of the butter.

Warm a large, deep saucepan over a high heat. When hot, add the remaining butter and the onion and fry for 5 minutes or until softened. Add the chorizo and cook for a further 5 minutes or until the orangey oils start to be released. Stir in the parsley, then remove from the heat and leave to cool for 10–15 minutes or until the mixture is cool enough to handle (and won't cook the eggs you're about to add).

Crumble the chestnuts into the pan, then add the breadcrumbs, chestnut purée, nutmeg and beaten eggs. Season generously with salt and pepper, then using your hands mix everything together. Press the mixture into the slow cooker dish. Cover with the lid and cook on low for 4–6 hours or until firm.

Spoon straight from the slow cooker dish to serve.

I ALSO LIKE...
to use diced, smoked streaky bacon instead of chorizo for a variation.

Christmas chutney

PREPARATION TIME: 15 MINUTES
COOKING TIME: 5–7 HOURS
MAKES 4 X 500ML (18FL OZ) JARS   VEGETARIAN

When I first graduated, I worked in a very posh London food hall. One of my first assignments was to develop some new products, the first of which was a Christmas chutney. It is still being sold to this day! Of course, I wouldn't dream of revealing the top-secret recipe in these pages, but here's a not-so-secret version!

750g (1lb 10oz) Bramley cooking apples, peeled, cored and sliced
Juice of 1 lemon
1 onion, peeled and diced
500g (1lb 2oz) fresh cranberries
200g (7oz) dried ready-to-eat figs, trimmed and diced
Finely grated zest and juice of 1 orange

200g (7oz) caster sugar
200g (7oz) soft light brown sugar
1 tsp ground allspice
½ tsp ground ginger
500ml (18fl oz) red wine vinegar
2 tsp sea salt

Place the apples in the slow cooker dish with the lemon juice and mix until the apples are coated. Add all the remaining ingredients and mix well. Poke any apple into the mixture so that it isn't in contact with the air (this will prevent the mixture from going too brown).

Cover with the lid and cook on high for 4 hours, then remove the lid and cook for a further 1–2 hours or until thick and the fruit has broken down.

Mix the chutney well with a wooden spoon, then divide between 4 sterilised 500ml (18fl oz) jars (see page 141–2). Seal and store in a cool, dark place for a minimum of two months or for up to a year (the longer the better to enable the flavours to mature).

I ALSO LIKE...
to vary the dried fruit in this recipe – prunes, dates and raisins all work well.

Bread sauce

PREPARATION TIME: 5 MINUTES
COOKING TIME: 3-4 HOURS
SERVES 12   VEGETARIAN

Either make the crumbs yourself or buy good-quality natural fresh crumbs – not the radioactive orange ones! Bread sauce should not boil, so the slow cooker is perfect for this.

25g (1oz) butter, plus extra for
  greasing
800g (1lb 12oz) fresh white
  breadcrumbs
1 litre (1¾ pints) whole milk
1 onion, peeled

6 cloves
2 bay leaves, broken
12 black peppercorns
Freshly grated nutmeg
Sea salt and freshly ground black
  pepper

Butter the inside of the slow cooker dish lightly. Tip the breadcrumbs into the slow cooker dish and add the milk.

Stud the onion with the cloves and place in the slow cooker together with the bay leaves and peppercorns. Cover with the lid and cook on low for 3–4 hours or until thick and fragrant.

Using tongs, remove and discard the onion, then remove and discard the bay leaves and peppercorns, if you wish. Add the butter and grated nutmeg and mix in with plenty of seasoning to taste.

FAB FOR THE FREEZER
Make and cook the sauce up to the end of paragraph 2, then remove and discard the onion and flavourings. Leave to cool and then freeze. Defrost thoroughly before reheating gently in a saucepan on the hob (never in the slow cooker). Beat in the butter, nutmeg and seasoning to taste.

Spiced mulled wine

PREPARATION TIME: 10 MINUTES
COOKING TIME: 2 HOURS
MAKES ABOUT 6 GLASSES   VEGETARIAN

This easy mulled wine recipe is given hidden flavour with the use of ginger wine, and happily uses redcurrant jelly for sweetness instead of mounds of sugar.

About 20 cloves
2 oranges, washed and dried
4 cinnamon sticks
75cl bottle good-quality, full-
  bodied red wine
150ml (5fl oz) ginger wine
3-4 tbsp redcurrant jelly, or to
  taste

Push the cloves – pointed end first – into the skin of one of the oranges. Peel the zest from the other orange with a vegetable peeler, then cut it in half and squeeze the juice.

Put the studded orange, zest and juice into the slow cooker dish, followed by the cinnamon, red and ginger wines. Cover with the lid and cook on high for 2 hours.

Add the redcurrant jelly to taste and stir until dissolved. Ladle into small cups or heatproof glasses to serve.

Cranberry and orange sauce

PREPARATION TIME: 5 MINUTES
COOKING TIME: 3 HOURS, PLUS COOLING
SERVES 8-10   VEGETARIAN

Easy as it is to make on the hob, using your slow cooker for cranberry sauce does at least free up some space, and will look after itself without concerns of boiling over or burning.

350g (12oz) fresh cranberries
200g (7oz) caster sugar, plus extra
 to taste
3 tbsp brandy
Juice of 1 orange

Rinse and drain the cranberries and place them in the slow cooker dish. Add the remaining ingredients and stir well. Cover with the lid and cook on low for 3 hours or until thickened and the fruit is breaking down.

Stir well and leave to cool for at least 10 minutes or until cool enough to taste. Add more sugar if needed. Transfer to a bowl and leave to cool completely. Keep covered in the fridge for up to a week. Stir well before serving.

FAB FOR THE FREEZER
The sauce can be frozen for up to a month. Defrost thoroughly before serving at room temperature.

Hot and spicy pomegranate cup

PREPARATION TIME: 5 MINUTES
COOKING TIME: 2-3 HOURS OR UNTIL NEEDED
SERVES 4   VEGETARIAN

This warm non-alcoholic drink is great for bonfire night, Christmas or wintry parties. This isn't difficult to make on the hob but in the slow cooker it will look after itself, keeping at a perfect temperature throughout. The dried red chilli gives the drink a warming spiciness as opposed to an overpowering wallop of heat.

500ml (18fl oz) pomegranate juice
500ml (18fl oz) apple juice
1 dried red chilli (optional)
2 cinnamon sticks
3 cloves
Juice and pared zest of 1 orange
50g (2oz) caster sugar

Mix all the ingredients together in the slow cooker dish. Cover with the lid and cook on low for 2–3 hours or until required.

Ladle into heatproof glasses or cups to serve.

I ALSO LIKE...
to add some brandy when serving a version with a kick.

Puddings

Six-hour cinnamon rice

PREPARATION TIME: 5 MINUTES

COOKING TIME: 6 HOURS

SERVES 8   VEGETARIAN

I absolutely love rice pudding! Here is an indulgent version using double cream. I am a fan of cinnamon and bay, but if you're not, then you can happily omit them without spoiling the flavour.

125g (4½oz) pudding or risotto
  rice
125g (4½oz) caster sugar
1 tsp ground cinnamon
1 litre (1¾ pints) whole milk
250ml (9fl oz) double cream, plus
  extra to serve
1 bay leaf, broken
50g (2oz) toasted almonds,
  chopped

Place a 2 litre (3½ pint) ovenproof dish in the slow cooker dish (or adjust the size and ingredients to fit your slow cooker dish).

Place the rice in the dish. Stir in the sugar, cinnamon, milk and cream, then add the bay leaf. Carefully pour enough boiling water around the outside to come about one-third of the way up the sides of the dish. Cover with the lid and cook on low for 6 hours or until the rice is tender and the cinnamon has crusted on the surface to form a brown skin.

Scatter the almonds over the dish and eat immediately with extra cream. Great with a fruit compote.

COOKING CONVENTIONALLY?
Cook in a 2 litre (3½ pint) ovenproof dish for 5 hours in an oven preheated to 140°C (275°F), Gas mark 1.

Rosy rhubarb roly-poly

PREPARATION TIME: 20-25 MINUTES
COOKING TIME: 2½-3½ HOURS, PLUS COOLING
SERVES 6-8

Roses... rhubarb... roly-poly... a few of my favourite things, so I just had to put them all together in a recipe!

200g (7oz) rhubarb, trimmed and chopped into 2cm (¾in) pieces
1 tbsp icing sugar
2 drops rose water, or to taste
Butter, for greasing
300g (10oz) self-raising flour, plus extra for dusting

150g (5oz) shredded suet (use vegetarian suet if preferred)
75g (3oz) caster sugar
Finely grated zest of 1 orange
175-200ml (6-7fl oz) milk

To make the filling, warm the rhubarb and icing sugar together in a saucepan over a medium heat until the fruit begins to soften. Increase the heat and bring to the boil. Cook for 5-10 minutes or until the juices thicken. Pour the mixture into a bowl and leave to cool for at least 30 minutes. Add the rose water sparingly, to taste.

Butter and lightly flour a large sheet of parchment paper, about 40 x 30cm (16 x 12in), and place it on a larger sheet of foil.

For the dough, mix together the flour, suet, caster sugar and orange zest in a large bowl. Stir in some milk until the mixture turns into soft dough. Gather together into a ball, but don't overwork or knead it as it will become tough.

On a lightly floured surface, roll the dough into a rectangle about 22 x 25cm (8½ x 10in). Spread with the cooled rhubarb mixture, leaving a 2cm (¾in) border around the edge. Moisten the border with the remaining milk. Then starting from one of the shorter ends of dough, start rolling the whole lot into a tight cylinder. With the seam underneath, lay the roly-poly in the centre of the parchment paper. Fold over the long paper and foil edges to seal, leaving enough space above the pudding to allow it to rise. Squeeze the paper ends together tightly to seal them.

Continued overleaf

Scrunch a large piece of foil into a thick cushion about the same size as the roly-poly. Place this in the base of the slow cooker dish and lay the parcel on top. Carefully pour enough boiling water around the outside to just cover the foil cushion and come to the base of the roly-poly. Cover with the lid and cook on high for 2–3 hours or until firm to the touch.

Remove from the slow cooker and leave to rest for 1–2 minutes before unwrapping. Use a serrated knife to cut it into thick slices and serve immediately with vanilla custard.

I ALSO LIKE...

to use this fruit purée on the base of a simple sponge mixture – see the orange and almond loaf cake recipe on page 166. Spoon the rhubarb purée onto the base before topping with the cake mixture.

Rich chocolate and hazelnut pudding

PREPARATION TIME: 15 MINUTES
COOKING TIME: 2 HOURS 10 MINUTES, PLUS PREHEATING
SERVES 8   VEGETARIAN

Our friends Sam and Toby are addicted to the hazelnut liqueur Frangellico, so this one is for them.

250g (9oz) unsalted butter, plus extra for greasing

200g (7oz) dark plain chocolate (at least 70% cocoa solids), broken into pieces

50g (2oz) chopped roasted hazelnuts

2 tbsp Frangellico liqueur (hazelnut liqueur), optional

100g (3½oz) cocoa powder, sifted

75g (3oz) self-raising flour, sifted

1 tsp baking powder

350g (12oz) caster sugar

5 medium eggs, beaten

Remove the slow cooker dish from the base. Butter the dish well and line with a double layer of parchment paper. Turn the slow cooker base (without the dish in it) on to high to preheat.

Melt the butter and chocolate in a large heatproof bowl over a saucepan of simmering water. Mix until smooth, then remove the bowl from the heat, add the hazelnuts and Frangellico (if using) and stir well.

In a separate bowl, mix the cocoa powder, flour, baking powder and sugar together. Add this to the melted chocolate mixture and stir well. Beat in the eggs until smooth.

Pour the mixture into the prepared slow cooker dish. Cover with the lid and carefully place the dish on the preheated slow cooker base. Cook for about 2 hours on low or until the centre is just set.

Remove from the base and leave to stand uncovered for about 10 minutes before serving warm with ice cream. Alternatively, leave to cool completely before cutting into chunky pieces and serving.

FAB FOR THE FREEZER
Cut the cooked and cooled pudding into portions and freeze. Defrost from frozen in the microwave for 1 minute on high or until hot and softened throughout.

Extra toffee banoffee pudding

PREPARATION TIME: 15 MINUTES

COOKING TIME: 2 HOURS, PLUS PREHEATING

SERVES 6–8   VEGETARIAN

I love banoffee pie, but this gooey, indulgent pudding takes my enjoyment to a whole new level!

75g (3oz) butter, melted, plus a
  little extra for greasing
125g (4½oz) self-raising flour
Pinch of salt
1½ tsp baking powder
100g (3½oz) golden caster sugar
2 bananas

250ml (9fl oz) milk
1 medium egg, lightly beaten
1 tsp vanilla extract
125g (4½oz) soft dark brown
  sugar
3 tbsp golden syrup
250ml (9fl oz) boiling water

Remove the slow cooker dish from the base and grease with a little butter. Turn the slow cooker base (without the dish in it) on to high to preheat.

Sift the flour, salt and baking powder into a bowl and add the sugar. In a small dish, mash one of the bananas with a fork and add it to the bowl together with the milk, melted butter, egg and vanilla and whisk well.

Cut the other banana into 2cm (¾in) pieces and arrange in a single layer in the base of the slow cooker dish. Pour the mixture over the top.

Place the brown sugar, golden syrup and boiling water in a bowl and stir until the sugar dissolves. Pour this mixture over the cake mix in the dish. Cover with the lid and carefully place the dish on the preheated slow cooker base. Cook on high for 2 hours.

Remove from the heat and leave to stand uncovered for 5–10 minutes before spooning into bowls. Serve with vanilla ice cream.

FAB FOR THE FREEZER
This pudding freezes brilliantly. Defrost thoroughly before reheating in the microwave for about 1 minute on high or until piping hot.

Mini coconut cups with mango and lime

PREPARATION TIME: 5 MINUTES
COOKING TIME: 2¼ HOURS
SERVES 8

VEGETARIAN

I use espresso cups for this recipe, but you could also use teacups or ramekins if you prefer.

1 x 400g (14oz) tin full-fat coconut
  milk
100g (3½oz) caster sugar
4 eggs

1 mango, peeled, stoned and cut
  into 5mm (¼in) cubes
Finely grated zest and juice of
  1 lime

Give the tin of coconut milk a good shake before opening it. Pour it into a large saucepan and warm over a medium heat. When it is just below boiling point remove it from the heat.

Meanwhile, whisk the sugar and eggs together in a large bowl. Gradually pour the warm coconut milk over the top, whisking as you pour. Place 8 espresso cups in the slow cooker dish, leaving a space to pour the water in.

Strain the coconut custard through a sieve into a jug and divide the custard between the cups. Carefully pour enough boiling water around the outside to come about one-third of the way up the sides of the cups. Cover with the lid and cook on low for 2 hours or until just set.

Carefully remove the cups from the water bath, place on a heatproof surface and leave to cool completely.

Meanwhile, place the mango in a bowl and stir in the lime zest and enough juice to taste. Set aside at room temperature until ready to serve.

Serve each coconut cup on a saucer with a spoonful of the colourful mango salad on top.

I ALSO LIKE...
to make these custards with whole milk instead of coconut milk, topping them with seasonal fresh fruit – strawberries and/or raspberries work well.

Chocolate bread and butter pudding

PREPARATION TIME: 20 MINUTES, PLUS SOAKING
COOKING TIME: 2 HOURS, PLUS PREHEATING
SERVES 6   VEGETARIAN

This recipe is a complete winner!

75g (3oz) butter, plus extra for
   greasing
150g (5oz) plain dark chocolate
   (at least 70% cocoa solids)
450ml (15fl oz) whipping cream
2 tbsp Marsala or brandy
   (optional)

100g (3½oz) caster sugar
4 medium eggs
200g (7oz) brioche loaf (chocolate
   chip brioche works well), cut
   into 8-10 thick slices

Butter the inside of the slow cooker dish. Place the chocolate, butter, cream, Marsala or brandy and sugar in a heatproof bowl over a saucepan of simmering water and melt. Once the chocolate has melted, mix well.

Whisk the eggs in a clean bowl, then slowly and steadily pour the chocolate mixture over the eggs, whisking continuously.

Spread about 5 tablespoons of the chocolate mixture over the base of the slow cooker dish. Overlap the brioche slices to cover the base. Pour the remaining chocolate mixture over the top and press the bread down into the liquid. Cover and leave in a cool place for at least 2 hours or for up to 24 hours (the longer the better!).

Preheat the slow cooker base on high for 30 minutes. Insert the slow cooker dish and cover with the lid. Cook on high for 2 hours or until just set in the centre.

Remove the pudding from the slow cooker and leave to rest for 10 minutes (use some kitchen paper to absorb any condensation on the surface of the pudding). Serve with lashings of double cream and some fruit compote if you're trying to convince yourself you're being good!

COOKING CONVENTIONALLY
Preheat the oven to 180°C (350°F), Gas mark 4. Place the mixture in a 23cm (9in) ovenproof dish and bake in the oven for 30-35 minutes.

St Clements cheesecake

PREPARATION TIME: 15 MINUTES
COOKING TIME: 2¼ HOURS, PLUS PREHEATING, COOLING AND CHILLING
SERVES 6–8   VEGETARIAN

This creamy cheesecake is studded with tangy citrus peel and tastes great. If you're not a fan of peel, though, just leave it out.

FOR THE CHEESECAKE:
375g (13oz) ricotta cheese
300g (10oz) full-fat cream cheese
2 tsp cornflour
200g (7oz) caster sugar
75g (3oz) cut mixed peel
 (optional)
4 eggs, beaten

4 eggs yolks, beaten
Finely grated zest of 2 lemons
 (preferably unwaxed)

FOR THE SYRUP:
225g (8oz) caster sugar
125ml (4fl oz) orange juice
1 lemon

Cover the base of the slow cooker dish with 1cm (½in) water, then cover with the lid and turn the slow cooker base on to high to preheat.

Butter a deep 18–20cm (7–8in) round non-stick cake tin and line the base and sides with parchment paper (make sure the tin fits into your slow cooker dish first – a 20cm/8in oval dish would work too if this fits your slow cooker more comfortably, or use 6 x 150ml/5fl oz ramekins).

To make the cheesecake, beat the ricotta and cream cheese together in a large bowl until smooth. Add the cornflour and sugar and mix well to combine. Fold in the dried fruit, whole eggs, egg yolks and the finely grated lemon zest.

Carefully place the cake tin in the slow cooker dish, cover with the lid and bake on high for 2 hours or until just set in the centre. Turn off and leave to cool in the water bath. Remove the tin from the slow cooker, place on a heatproof surface and leave to cool completely. When cold, cover and chill in the fridge overnight.

To make the syrup, place the sugar and orange juice in a heavy-based saucepan over a low heat and stir to dissolve. Increase the heat and bring to the boil. Using a zester, remove the zest from the lemon in long strands and add these to the boiling syrup. Boil for 10–12 minutes or until syrupy. Remove from the heat and leave to stand for 5 minutes before serving drizzled over generous slices of the cheesecake.

Middle Eastern fruit and nut salad

PREPARATION TIME: 5 MINUTES
COOKING TIME: 4–6 HOURS
SERVES 6–8   VEGETARIAN

Use dried apricots and prunes for this tasty recipe, not the ready-to-eat varieties – these have already been soaked and will disintegrate during cooking.

400g (14oz) dried apricots
100g (3½oz) prunes
100g (3½oz) raisins
100g (3½oz) blanched almonds
50g (2oz) pistachios
Juice of 1 orange
2 tbsp clear honey, or to taste
Orange blossom water, to taste
Pomegranate seeds, to serve

Place the dried fruits and nuts in the slow cooker dish. Pour in just enough cold water to come one-third of the way up the fruit. Drizzle over the orange juice and honey. Cover with the lid and cook on low for 4–6 hours or until thickened and syrupy.

Add enough orange blossom water to taste, and some more honey if required. Scatter over the pomegranate seeds and serve over vanilla ice cream.

I ALSO LIKE...
to cook fresh apricots in the same way when they're in season, but I leave out the prunes if I'm doing this.

Crunchy vanilla crème caramels

PREPARATION TIME: 15 MINUTES

COOKING TIME: 2 HOURS 20 MINUTES, PLUS COOLING AND CHILLING

SERVES 4   VEGETARIAN

These dainty desserts are a variation on a traditional crème caramel.

100g (3½oz) granulated sugar

150ml (5fl oz) cold water

350ml (12fl oz) milk (skimmed is fine if you want to cut down on fat)

200ml (7fl oz) double cream

1 tsp vanilla extract

2 medium eggs

3 medium egg yolks

25g (1oz) caster sugar

Line a baking sheet with a piece of non-stick parchment paper. Set 4 x 250ml (9fl oz) ovenproof teacups to one side (or use ramekins of the same size).

Place the granulated sugar in a heavy-based saucepan together with the water and warm over a high heat. Do not stir the mixture but swirl the pan occasionally until the sugar dissolves. Bring to the boil and cook for 7–10 minutes or until golden.

Pour a quarter of the caramel onto the prepared baking sheet and leave to cool completely. When cold, cover and leave at room temperature until needed.

Meanwhile, spoon the remaining caramel into the teacups. Don't wash up the pan, as you will need it for the custard mixture.

Pour the milk, cream and vanilla into the caramel saucepan. Warm over a medium heat for 10 minutes, stirring frequently, until any caramel has dissolved, and the mixture is just below boiling point. Remove from the heat and leave to stand while you prepare the eggs.

Place the eggs, egg yolks and caster sugar in a large bowl and whisk together well. Slowly pour the hot milk mixture over the top, whisking continuously as you pour. Strain the mixture through a sieve into a large jug, then pour into the caramel-lined cups.

Place the cups in the base of the slow cooker dish and carefully pour enough boiling water around the outside to come about one-third of the way up the sides of the cups.

Continued overleaf

Cover with the lid and cook on low for 2½ hours (or on high for 1½ hours) or until the custard is just set in the centre.

Remove the cups from the water bath and leave to cool completely on a heatproof surface before chilling in the fridge overnight.

Just before eating, place the now solid caramel on the baking sheet in a freezer bag and bash with a wooden rolling pin to break into shards.

Loosen the edges of the custards with the tip of a sharp knife, then invert onto plates. Scatter the caramel shards over the tops before serving.

I ALSO LIKE...
adding a touch of brandy or Cointreau to the custard before pouring it into the cups.

Double chocolate and pear pudding

PREPARATION TIME: 10 MINUTES

COOKING TIME: 1½ HOURS, PLUS PREHEATING

SERVES 4   VEGETARIAN

This intensely chocolaty pudding with pear is made with a sauce on the top and sponge underneath. As it cooks it magically swaps around, leaving a pool of gooey chocolate in the bottom of the dish.

50g (2oz) butter, melted and cooled, plus extra for greasing

100g (3½oz) self-raising flour

3 tbsp cocoa powder, plus extra for dusting

125g (4½oz) golden caster sugar

1 medium egg

4 tbsp milk

1 ripe pear, peeled, cored and diced

50g (2oz) soft dark brown sugar

Cover the base of the slow cooker dish with 1cm (½in) water, then cover with the lid and turn the slow cooker base on to high to preheat. Butter a 1 litre (1¾ pint) ovenproof serving dish (make sure it will fit into your slow cooker dish first, or use four 200ml (7fl oz) ovenproof ramekins).

Sift the flour and half of the cocoa powder into a large bowl. Add the caster sugar and mix together.

Whisk the cooled, melted butter, egg and milk together in a small bowl, then pour over the flour mixture and whisk together well. Fold in the pear and spoon the mixture into the prepared serving dish.

In a separate bowl, mix the remaining cocoa and the brown sugar together. Sprinkle this over the mixture in the serving dish. Carefully place the pudding in the warm water in the slow cooker. Spoon 4 tablespoons of freshly boiled water evenly over the top of the pudding and pour any remainder around the outside to come one-third of the way up the sides of the pudding. Cover with the lid and cook on high for 1½ hours or until a skewer inserted halfway into the pudding comes out clean.

Remove the pudding from the slow cooker. Dust with more cocoa powder and serve immediately with crème fraîche or ice cream. Best eaten straight away.

Sticky plum cake

PREPARATION TIME: 15 MINUTES
COOKING TIME: 2 HOURS, PLUS PREHEATING
SERVES 8   VEGETARIAN

This moist cake is great eaten cold on its own or warm as a pudding with custard.

200g (7oz) softened butter, plus
  extra for greasing
100g (3½oz) caster sugar, plus
  1 tbsp extra for dusting
6 plums, halved and stoned
100g (3½oz) self-raising flour

1 tsp baking powder
100g (3½oz) ground almonds
100g (3½oz) soft dark brown
  sugar
4 medium eggs, beaten

Remove the slow cooker dish from the base. Turn the slow cooker base (without the dish in it) on to high to preheat. Butter and line the sides and base of the slow cooker dish with parchment paper, paying particular attention to the corners. Dust the base of the dish with the tablespoon of caster sugar.

Place the plums flat side down in the slow cooker dish.

Sift the flour and baking powder into a large bowl. Add all the remaining ingredients and mix until smooth. Don't worry if it curdles slightly, it won't affect the finished cake. Pour over the plums and insert the slow cooker dish on the preheated base. Cover with the lid and cook on high for 2 hours or until the edges are springy to the touch (the middle will still be soft).

Remove the dish from the base and leave to stand on a heatproof surface with the lid on for 30 minutes. Carefully invert onto a plate and remove the parchment paper. Eat warm or cold.

I ALSO LIKE...
using halved apricots instead of plums.

Apricot upside-down cake

PREPARATION TIME: 15 MINUTES
COOKING TIME: 2 HOURS 10 MINUTES, PLUS PREHEATING
SERVES 6-8   VEGETARIAN

This easy recipe can be eaten as a cake or a dessert.

100g (3½oz) butter, softened, plus
  extra for greasing
1 x 400g (14oz) tin apricot halves
  in syrup
200g (7oz) caster sugar

4 eggs, separated
1 tsp almond extract
150g (5oz) plain flour
2 tsp baking powder

Remove the slow cooker dish from the base and turn the slow cooker on to high to preheat. Butter the slow cooker dish and line the base and sides with parchment paper, paying particular attention to the corners.

Strain the apricots through a sieve and set the syrup aside. Arrange the apricots in a single layer, flat side down, in the slow cooker dish.

Cream the butter and sugar together in a large bowl until light and fluffy, then add the egg yolks one at a time, beating well between each addition. Mix in the almond extract.

Sift the flour and baking powder into the bowl and beat until the mixture is smooth.

In a clean bowl, whisk the egg whites until stiff. Add a spoonful to the almond mixture and fold in gently to loosen. Fold in the remaining whites. Spoon the mixture into the prepared slow cooker dish. Cover with the lid and place on the preheated base. Cook on high for 2 hours or until spongy to the touch.

Invert onto a plate and remove the parchment paper.

Pour the reserved syrup into a small saucepan and bring to the boil over a high heat. Cook for 5-10 minutes or until reduced and thickened. Brush the thick syrup over the warm cake as a glaze. Serve in slices either hot or cold.

FAB FOR THE FREEZER
This cake freezes really well. I usually freeze it in portions and take them out as I need them. Defrost thoroughly before eating.

Orange and almond loaf cake

PREPARATION TIME: 10 MINUTES
COOKING TIME: 3-3½ HOURS
SERVES 4

VEGETARIAN

Make sure the loaf tin will fit in the slow cooker first; alternatively, if you have a smaller machine, make this cake in ramekins or individual pudding basins (adjust the cooking time accordingly).

100g (3½oz) butter, softened, plus
  extra for greasing
100g (3½oz) golden caster sugar
2 medium eggs, beaten
50g (2oz) self-raising flour

50g (2oz) ground almonds
½ tsp baking powder
4 tbsp semi-skimmed milk
Finely grated zest of 1 orange
50g (2oz) toasted, flaked almonds

Butter a non-stick 500g (1lb 2oz) loaf tin with butter and line the base with parchment paper. Place a trivet or upturned saucer in the base of the slow cooker and pour enough cold water around it to just cover the top, about 250ml (9fl oz).

Cream the butter and sugar together in a large bowl until light and fluffy. Slowly add the eggs, beating well between each addition. Fold in the flour, ground almonds and baking powder, then slowly stir in the milk and the orange zest.

Scatter the flaked almonds over the base of the prepared tin, then spoon the sponge into the tin and level the surface with the back of the spoon. Cover tightly with a lightly buttered piece of foil, butter side down.

Place in the slow cooker on top of the trivet or saucer and cover with the lid. Cook for 3-3½ hours or until risen and spongy to the touch.

Remove from the slow cooker and leave to stand on a heatproof surface for a minute or so. Run a sharp knife around the sponge before inverting onto a wire rack and leave to cool completely. Using a serrated knife, cut into thick slices and serve with lashings of cream or crème fraîche.

I ALSO LIKE...
to vary this recipe with fruit instead of the flaked almonds – scatter 50g (2oz) berries, such as raspberries, over the base before topping with the cake mixture.

Real vanilla custard

PREPARATION TIME: 5 MINUTES

COOKING TIME: 2-3 HOURS

SERVES 6-8   VEGETARIAN

Real custard is easy enough to make on the hob but it needs constant attention and stirring for a good 10-15 minutes before it starts to thicken. This method looks after itself in the slow cooker.

1 vanilla pod
1 tsp cornflour
300ml (10fl oz) double cream
3 large egg yolks
25g (1oz) caster sugar

Using the tip of a small sharp knife, cut the vanilla pod in half lengthways. Scrape the seeds out of the pod and place them in a 1 litre (1¾ pint) heatproof bowl (check that the bowl fits into your slow cooker first) together with the now empty pod.

Place the cornflour in a small dish and mix in a little of the cream, until there are no lumps. Pour this into the bowl with the vanilla, add the remaining cream, egg yolks and sugar and whisk well.

Cut a piece of parchment paper into a round just larger than the top of the bowl. Dampen under cold water and scrunch it up into a loose ball (this will make it easier to handle). Place the drained disc of parchment directly on the surface of the egg mixture, pushing it down around the edges to create a seal.

Place a trivet or upturned saucer in the base of the slow cooker dish and pour in just enough cold water to cover it and position the bowl on top. Cover with the lid and cook on low for 2-3 hours or until thickened.

Carefully remove the bowl from the slow cooker and place on a heatproof surface. Whisk well and remove the vanilla pod before serving.

I ALSO LIKE...
to keep the vanilla pod (it will still have plenty of flavour), rinse it in some clean water and dry with kitchen paper, then embed it in a jar of caster sugar, cocoa or coffee to impart a gorgeous vanilla flavour.

Amazing hot chocolate sauce

PREPARATION TIME: 5 MINUTES
COOKING TIME: 1–2 HOURS
SERVES 6 AS A CHOCOLATE POT AND 8–10 AS A SAUCE   VEGETARIAN

This super-easy sauce is a chocoholic's dream! It's rich and delicious – perfect for spooning, drizzling or dipping, and if you leave it to go cold it will solidify into a dense, truffle-like mousse.

200g (7oz) plain dark chocolate, broken into pieces
100g (3½oz) milk chocolate, broken
6 marshmallows, roughly chopped

300ml (10fl oz) half-fat crème fraîche
150ml (5fl oz) skimmed milk
2 tbsp Baileys liqueur (optional)

Place all the ingredients in a heatproof bowl that will fit into your slow cooker dish. Pour enough cold water into the slow cooker dish around the bowl to come about one-third of the way up the sides of the bowl. Cover with the lid and cook on low for 1 hour.

Beat well to combine and then leave on the warming function for up to an hour before use. Spoon over sundaes or profiteroles, or dip in fruit and biscuits as a sweet fondue.

I ALSO LIKE...
to pour the mixture into little ramekins or espresso cups and leave to cool. The sauce will set into an intense, gooey chocolate pot.

Index

Recipes

Main ingredients

Acknowledgements

My sincere thanks go once again to my editor Lizzy Gray, for being brave enough to commission me and for guiding me through the process with care, humour and patience. Thanks too to Susanna Abbott for taking the manuscript through to print.

Thank you to the fabulous Jenny White, for being so lovely and for making the food in the photos look so gorgeously tantalising; thanks also to Steve Baxter for taking the shots.

I have tested my recipes in a bank of eight Crockpot slow cookers, most of them kindly donated by Crockpot and Pittilla PR – thank you for your generosity. Thanks also to Waitrose and, in particular, to Gary Grace, for the very generous provision of fabulous meat with which to test my recipes. It was a joy to work with such wonderful ingredients and I hope this book will encourage more people to cook with forgotten cuts, in turn helping British farmers to make a better living for themselves.

My love and thanks go as ever to my wonderful, irreplaceable family – Mummy, Daddy and the world's best bro Simon; but thanks especially to my gorgeous husband Rupert who is always patiently and lovingly there, and who was particularly wonderful during the many frantic moments as the deadline approached on this book (a mere 7 days before our wedding day!). We made it, honey, and I am so proud and lucky to be your wife.

Finally, I want to dedicate this book to two very special ladies who have taught me so much over the last 20 years, both about food and how to be a better person. Ev and Sue – you're brill and lovely. This one's for you! x x

About the author

Kate Bishop is a successful food writer and stylist. Her love of food led her to enter the acclaimed Young Cook of Britain competition at the age of 14. Katie beat over 32,000 entrants to win, giving her the opportunity to work alongside some of the Britain's most renowned chefs.

Katie has worked as a chef around the world but is now based in London. She regularly writes for food magazines, contributes to online sites, pens bestselling cookbooks and appears as a guest chef on TV.